MOURINHO
HAPPY & SPECIAL

NUNO LUZ
LUÍS MIGUEL PEREIRA

MOURINHO
HAPPY & SPECIAL

PRIME BOOKS

MOURINHO
Happy & Special
by Luís Miguel Pereira and Nuno Luz

© For the text, Luís Miguel Pereira and Nuno Luz
© For the pictures, Jorge Monteiro (Gestifute)
© For the cover picture, Getty Images
© For this edition, Prime Books

This edition first published in the UK in 2014 by
Prime Books, Lda.
Rua Brito Camacho, Lt 43 – 1º Esq.
S. João do Estoril
2765-457 Estoril
Portugal
www.primebooks.pt

Originaly published in Portugal in November 2011 by Prime Books

Editor: Jaime Abreu
Translation: Sintagma Traduções
Design and artwork production: Arco da Velha
Typesetting: Paulo Resende
Print and Binding: Cafilesa

ISBN: 978-989-655-196-4

Legal Deposit: 373934/14

I'm a genuine Mourinho fan. Because he's passionate, because he's a great motivator and because, despite his eagerness, he's very vulnerable. I'm convinced that when he makes a mistake he feels profoundly remorseful. I believe Mourinho is vulnerable and this vulnerability makes him very human. **JULIO IGLESIAS**

To my wife and children, I was away for many days to accomplish this project. A special thanks to José Mourinho for having trusted me to make the documentary on his career that resulted in this book.

NUNO LUZ

To both my Quicas, my Tomás and my Martim.

Thanks to José Mourinho, who allowed me to fulfil the dream of writing a book about him, the best coach of all time.

LUÍS MIGUEL PEREIRA

Dedication by Jorge Mendes

FOREWORD

I don't have the slightest doubt: if I were a player, my dream would be to have José Mourinho as my coach throughout my whole career, or at least for a good part of it. Why? Because that would ensure that my best qualities would be stretched to the maximum and my weaknesses would be reduced and transformed into something useful for myself and for my team. So I would become a better player than I was before working with him. Besides this certainty, I'd also know that with him I'd win many more titles than with anyone else. This is nothing new: José Mourinho has the innate ability to get the maximum performance out of each and every player, whether he's the best in the world or the typical average player.

There are countless examples of expressions of recognition. Not one player, active or retired, points a finger of resentment or dissatisfaction at him. On the contrary, the football universe is full of examples of voices expressing their gratitude, listing his vast capacities and shedding a tear when they lose him as their leader, upset by a marked feeling of loss. Whether they are the most troublesome or the most peaceful of professionals. On the other hand, Mourinho is and will continue to be the solution to all the problems of the club that hires him. In contrast, clubs feel his exit immeasurably, because his heritage is too much for his successors. This has happened in every club he's been in. And I'm sure that it will carry on this way, because we're talking about an unrivalled phenomenon when it comes to the art of coaching. That's one of his secrets. But he's got more, many more.

José Mourinho isn't just a coach – and as a coach he's the best and most complete coach ever. He is simultaneously a human resources manager, a psychologist, a pedagogue, a disciplinarian, a leader. He has the capacity to bring together a vast group of personalities, moods and wills, getting them all to share the same ideology, principles and rules. He has the ability to metamorphose differences, turning them into strength, power and fortitude. Whether he is facing the most attainable objective or the boldest challenge, his extreme confidence and belief in himself make him believe everything is possible. On top of that, he manages to get the same feeling across to everyone surrounding him. That's why there's no such thing as insurmountable obstacles for him. His players are imbued with this spirit and would give their life for him.

José Mourinho could just be the best in terms of leadership, or the best as far as tactics are concerned, or the best regarding strategy or organisation, or the best psychologically speaking, or the most intelligent one. But no. An assessment of all these characteristics of his places Mourinho undeniably at an enormous distance from anyone else: he is the best of all times. Mourinho marked Portuguese football; he marked English football; he marked Italian football; he marked Spanish football. World football at the highest level lived one era before him, another with him, and will surely live yet another, far poorer, after him. However much we try to find someone like him, we can't, and we won't in the next 500 years. Because José Mourinho is, and always will be, unique. To compare him to certain other geniuses would only make them stop being looked upon as such.

JORGE MENDES

ORGANIZATION...

I'll always remember the times we worked together. They were the best of my career. Thanks for everything.

PAULO FERREIRA

I'm a young player and Mourinho knows what I need. He's turning me into a more complete player.

RAPHAEL VARANE

I wake up at 7 o'clock and I arrive at the stadium at 8.15. Before the training session starts I have two hours of complete calm, in the silence of my office, to carefully prepare the working session which is specified according to the analysis that I and my assistants carried out regarding this micro-cycle at the end of the previous week. These are two hours of fruitful solitude, mixed with the whisper of the cleaning ladies and the sound of their mops.

Before the training session I still have time for a brief meet with my scouts for a perfect identification of the next opponent; with the guy in charge of the grass, to check the good state of the training field, taking into account the weather forecast for the weekend; with the training kit staff; with the doctor to evaluate the clinical situation and to define the plan for the injured players and for those players in the process of integration.

Roughly two hours of training, followed by a meeting to assess it. Then another meeting with the person in charge of the press to define a later meeting between the professionals and the media.

Next is a meeting with the chief executive of the SAD and his secretary, to analyse a multitude of aspects and, finally, just one moment to call home where the kids have already arrived from school and are having lunch.

Next, five minutes to relax walking quietly to Colombo, where our staff is having lunch, and then back to the stadium where a second training session fills my afternoon, or a few more hours in the office. Between viewing tapes, drawing up the development plan for youth football and preparing the next season, the afternoon flies by. Before leaving the stadium I pass by the upper floors to meet with the interested people at the top of SLB's SAD. Finally, the quick drive to Setúbal, where my wife, Matilde and Zé Mário are waiting for me to have supper, and where the love of a happy family is rejuvenating (…)."

This chronicle was written by José Mourinho himself, on 25th October 2000, for the Portuguese electronic sports newspaper "Mais Futebol". Mourinho was portraying the routine of a head coach – his routine – at the service of Benfica: method, order and smoothness are what stands out from the text.

This is how it went on his first day as coach. That's how it goes, all these years later. Mourinho is like an octopus whose many tentacles literally touch all areas: planning, training, media, state of the grass, observation of opponents, youth football, weather, the SAD… absolutely everything. Maniche, who was present at this first training session and later accompanied the Portuguese coach in FC Porto and in Chelsea, confirms that "He was just another player, one more of us, but at the same time he was a leader."

He likes to participate in everything. He's groundsman, chauffeur, security… he likes to control everything in minute detail. He thinks about the team 24 hours a day. **MANICHE**

Organisation is almost an obsessive issue for José Mourinho. That's why he's the first to arrive at the training centre; that's why he's the one who spends most time at the work place; that's why he thinks football day and night. The result is: training sessions prepared to the smallest detail; solutions to every problem the game poses; and victories, many of them.

This wholehearted availability has been there from the very start. Álvaro Braga Júnior, the first sports director in José Mourinho's career, in Benfica, remembers an episode that describes well this limitless devotion: "I had dinner with Mourinho the day before his presentation to the press and on that day he immediately made a request. Despite having his family quite close by, in Setúbal, he told me he preferred to live in Lisbon because like that he could devote himself one hundred per cent to Benfica, without the pressure of family and friends. So he stayed at a hotel in Lisbon and, apart from the training sessions, the only thing he did was watch videos and study opponents. I can witness that because I saw it and, at the beginning, I very often had lunch and dinner with him." Mourinho lost the first game of his career, against Boavista, by 1-0. And Braga Júnior says that even in that moment of failure, Mourinho's organisation stood out: "We lost in the way he said it was possible we would lose."

TOTAL INFORMATION

Frank Lampard was impressed when he entered José Mourinho's office in London for the first time: "He's got all the months filled up, the whole season planned, all the training sessions and all that's fundamental for the players' constant evolution. He's the full works!"

The Portuguese coach plans the season in detail, according to the scheduled games, to the players available, to which of them are in top shape, and so on. The number of variables considered in the planning reduces the margin of error. That's why Mourinho is rarely wrong. As far as possible, everything is predicted.

"Work" is a sacred word for the coach. Whoever doesn't understand that will have great difficulty in jumping on the train. The players are also chosen with the same criterion in mind: "Chelsea's success, for example, started being built by the type of players Mourinho brought with him", guarantees Pinto da Costa, president of FC Porto. "I remember that, during our early talks, hiring Beckham and Roberto Carlos came up. And straight away he said no way, he preferred players like Ricardo Carvalho and Paulo Ferreira, players he knew and who would help the team to win, not to sell shirts. There's no question about the value of Beckham or Roberto Carlos, that they're extraordinary, but they wouldn't have the ambition he wanted", concludes the president of the Dragons.

Mourinho doesn't tolerate truants nor does he sponsor loiterers. He provides the athletes with organised working conditions, but he demands that they do their part.

When you see him arriving at 7.30h or 8.00h in the morning, after dropping off his kids at school, you know work is going to be serious. He goes on the pitch and says: "You're going to train for one hour and during one hour you've got to give it your everything." It's all there... everything in José Mourinho is perfect. **JOHN TERRY**

His dossiers with all the indispensable information on the opponents are famous. The players are amazed with the level of detail revealed in the documents: "On Tuesday, when we got there, we'd have a dossier with everything you can imagine on the opponent: free kicks, corner kicks, throw-ins... the works. Even details about who was the most undisciplined player and the best way to provoke him so as to make the opposing team weaker. It was a remarkable thing", says Costinha.

This level of organisation made Maniche feel responsible: "That way, he passed the responsibility onto us. From then on it was up to each one of us to study the opponent; it was all there for us. And for players who want to become coaches one day, they've got a brilliant example of how the work should be done." As Jorge Costa states: "If we didn't win the game there was only one explanation: we hadn't been competent on the pitch." In other words, "the key lesson was understanding that you've always got to work more, never slow down and never neglect the details", concludes Diego Milito.

This method brings comfort to Mourinho's players and creates huge difficulties for his opponents. Sometimes, when he had to play against teams trained by the Portuguese coach, Cristiano Ronaldo felt that:

He studies his opponents better than the other coaches. He knows the weak and the strong points of all the players and of all the teams. Obviously that shows on the pitch. His players turn up with the clear notion that they know their opponent. When I played against him I had great difficulty in 'relaxing' my football. **CRISTIANO RONALDO**

Mourinho's commitment is the same in any circumstance. The name of the opponents doesn't numb his determination, "he prepares a Cup match, against a third division team, with the same engagement and detail he puts into a Champions League final", assures Jorge Costa.

For each case, Mourinho has more than one solution. He presents the players with expected, anticipated and already solved scenarios. Vítor Baía has a very clear example of this extreme organisation:

"Before one game at Luz stadium he went as far as naming Benfica's 'eleven' and what would happen if we scored first: 'You already know that Camacho always goes and gets Sokota when he's at a disadvantage, so this is what we'll have to do…' And he went on: 'Now imagine one of their players is expelled, in that case we're going to act this way…' " Coincidentally, or not, in that game everything Mourinho said in the training session happened: FC Porto scored first, with Deco, in the 36th minute; Camacho's first replacement put Tom Sokota in the game, replacing Zahovic, in the 46th minute; and Ricardo Rocha, Benfica's centre-back, was expelled in the 70th minute. FC Porto won 0-1.

Milito recalls a similar episode, against Chelsea, in the Champions League 2009/2010 quarter-finals. Inter brought an insufficient advantage to London, 2-1, the result of the first leg. "Before the match he was very clear: "If we don't commit fouls in dangerous zones, if we don't suffer goals from dead-ball situations… we will not only pass this round but we'll also win the game."" And that is what happened. Inter committed very few fouls and won 0-1 (goal by Eto'o). A perfect game. "These things really make an impression on us because everything he said, happened", adds Milito. It's not magic, it's work. It's not luck, it's organisation. "Everything we did in our daily lives had to do with the competition, everything we did in training was what happened in the game", Vítor Baía concludes.

THE "OTHER" TECHNICAL TEAM

José Mourinho's technical team is not just a matter of the assistants who accompany him in the training sessions. There is another group of "invisible" professionals, trained to spy on the opponents' every movement. They are a kind of special agents, the 007's of the Portuguese coach.

The mission of this group is to provide information as detailed as possible. Mourinho doesn't want to know how difficult it is and doesn't intend to worry about the issue. So he delegated the coordination of this task to José Morais. Interestingly, the coach began his career in Spain, as a scout for Atlético de Madrid, and then worked at all four corners of the globe (Portugal, Germany, Sweden, Saudi Arabia, Jordan, Tunisia and Yemen) as head coach, assistant coach or acting as observer and scout.

Today José Morais is coordinating a team of six, among them observers, image editors and graphic designers. This group of professionals is responsible for preparing reports and producing videos with information on the opponents' assets, weak points, aspects to look into, and so on. Each opponent justifies at least four live observations and another two on video.

But this espionage goes beyond the matches. The information is completed with news from the papers, observation of training sessions and even phone calls to people close to the opponents. "Often we resort to the everyday work done by journalists, because it is a credible source of information. We find out what they say throughout the week, the probable team, the injury of player A, B or C, what they did while training and the result of that training. The press conference with the coach also sort of expresses his own feelings about how the match is going to go... all this allows us to draw conclusions about the way the opponent may be approaching the game. Then we have our network of contacts which we've created over the years. You always know someone who knows someone else who can help you indirectly with information about a player or the team. For example, we're going to play against Benfica, and if a certain player is going to play, I call a friend of a friend of his and, in a roundabout way, I can always discover what I want. Observing training is harder, because we don't always have access to it, and besides, it so happens that I'm already well known. I can't go to the opponents' training sessions because they might recognise me. But we always send someone who can carry out this task discretely", says José Morais.

The current assistant coach and head of the scouting department of Real Madrid met José Mourinho in the year 2000, when he was coaching Benfica. At the time José Morais was in charge of the reds' B team and he remembers he was particularly impressed with the level of organisation van Gaal's former assistant showed from day one at Luz. Well above all the others he'd met at the club.

Mourinho values every detail because you can only ask for results from the team when everyone is working at the same level. Often he's the first to propose getting some last-minute information, which can then make the difference in preparing the game. **JOSÉ MORAIS**

In 11 years, José Mourinho's scouting department underwent radical changes. Early on, the Portuguese coach realised the importance of a strong scouting area in a top technical team. He must have understood this immediately when preparing the first game as head coach, in Benfica. The opponent was Boavista and, as always, the club sent one of its scouts to make a report. In the notes he took down, the scout forgot to mention the presence of Erwin Sanchez, "only" the most influential player of the team. José Mourinho was furious with this flaw, which he considered unacceptable in a club with Benfica's status. Faced with such a serious mistake, he decided to put forever his technical team in charge of scouting the opponents, under his own supervision. Not least because this was a matter he knew inside out, thanks to the work he did in Barcelona as Louis van Gaal's assistant.

At Benfica he solved the problem like this: he immediately decided to pay from his own pocket for someone from outside the club, but whom he trusted, to start producing reports on the opponents. After this episode, opponent scouting became a priority for Mourinho for the rest of his career.

Also while at Benfica, and with the information gathered by this trusted collaborator, it was José Mourinho himself who prepared the players' presentation. Carlos Mozer, his then assistant coach, recalls the "existence of a board, on an easel, in the Benfica changing rooms, where he wrote down all the opponent's data, on several giant sheets." Detailed, accurate, surgical information. The same principles that his collaborators – André Villas-Boas and José Morais – would later adopt when they took on the scouting department.

During his periods with Benfica and, before those, with União de Leiria, in the first two years of his career, José Mourinho resorted to occasional collaborators to fill up the scouting department. Stabilisation and sustained development only came about in 2002, in FC Porto, with the integration of André Villa-Boas. The club already had a scouting department, which actually worked well, but Mourinho – through Villas-Boas – introduced a small revolution in it: he radically changed the way of observing the opponents, of systemising information and of presenting the work.

Even when with Inter Milan, conditions were not as good as the Portuguese coach now has in Real Madrid. José Morais coordinated a team of four scouts, all of them freelancers, who watched at least

four of the opponent's games and produced the reports. Morais watched at least one of those matches live and drew up a summary of all the information in one document. For the video area, Inter had only one image editor who carried out the technical editing work. "All the graphic work and inserting text was done by me", explains José Morais.

PERSONALISED VIDEOS

Video is a precious weapon in José Mourinho's work. At a first stage, it is through video that the coach meets the opponents and prepares tasks suited to the field work. "The players exercise based on the information resulting from that viewing and on the strategies for the game. It is a truly comprehensive process that allows our players to gain in-depth knowledge of the opponent", says Rui Faria.

At a second stage, the utility of video reaches the players directly. They are prepared with detail, selectively, but, as Rui Faria explains, also with well-defined rules regarding length: "The videos shown to the players are never long, 10 minutes at most, so as not to cause mental fatigue. We know from experience that, after 10 minutes, it's difficult to keep the players concentrated. We make a strict selection of information so as to keep them motivated." Often, as José Morais explains, it is Mourinho himself who edits the video material resulting from the scouting. "It's up to Zé to decide whether to use all of it or if there are less interesting aspects that can be eliminated."

The contents are a real "amusement park" to any player the least bit interested in football and with the desire to win. "There are personalised videos. For example, defenders have images of forwards; forwards have images of the goalkeeper and of the defenders... When we step on the pitch it's as if we've known our direct opponent for years", says Jorge Costa.

Pinto da Costa, president of FC Porto in Mourinho's first European win, has proof of this minutia at home: "We blindly believed we were going to win the UEFA Cup final against Celtic Glasgow, because everything had been prepared with the utmost rigour. With much esteem I have kept the final's board, where he had everything outlined, the players' heights, their positions, who marked whom... he offered me that board with a dedication."

That's why José Mourinho is the calmest man in the world before any clash.

Even if it was an important, tense game, José was always really calm and relaxed. But that happened because he was better prepared for that game than anyone else. When the opponent made a replacement, he'd respond with an even better one. That was the result of his preparation, of his knowledge of the opponent and of his own team. **PETER KENYON**

The game in the second leg of the Champions 2009/10 semi-final with Barcelona, at Camp Nou, was emblematic. Inter had beaten the Catalans 3-1, in San Siro, but this result was far from comfortable. It became even worse when Thiago Motta was expelled in the 28th minute of the first part, leaving Inter with ten players. A full hour of massacre could be anticipated at Júlio César's goal, in a hostile atmosphere, facing what many considered the best team in the world. The typical Nerazzurri supporter would have felt everything collapse around him, but for the Inter players it was just one more obstacle on their path to success: "We'd already come up against Barcelona in the group stage and lost 2-0, at Camp Nou, because we'd played badly. When we returned for the semi-finals, Mourinho knew exactly how we should act to get to the final. We knew exactly what to do. It's impossible to 'cheat him' twice. He prepared this match really well", says Diego Milito. José Mourinho confirms this:

Before the Champions semi-final, against Barcelona, my assistants and I spent the night at Inter's training centre "devouring" videos and preparing for the game. **MOURINHO**

Proof that… Mourinho doesn't sleep.

MOURINHO'S CRUTCHES

Two men have been José Mourinho's unconditional shadows from day one: Rui Faria and Silvino Louro. These assistants have been together for over ten years, sharing many triumphs and a few anguishes. It is also on these two men that a good part of José Mourinho's organisational obsession rests.

Silvino stresses the coach's permanent requital, even from his assistants: "Zé is really demanding with whoever works with him. No-one can stop or get comfortable. We have to be up-to-date and at our best every single day." The goalkeeper coach had already been working for two years when he began to work with Mourinho, but this last decade just doesn't compare: "He transformed me into an immeasurably more qualified coach, without a doubt."

The common history between Silvino and Mourinho goes back to their childhood, to the streets of Setúbal. It is a relationship made of personal and even familiar affection. But that doesn't mean more professional time off. With Rui Faria it's different. They met in Barcelona, when Mourinho was Robson's assistant and Faria was for studying for his sports and physical education MA. He got his degree in 1999 and sent the final work to José Mourinho's Catalan mailbox. "I did that with several coaches I knew and Mourinho was the only one who called to thank me and give his opinion about my work", says Rui Faria. In the course of that phone call, and amidst several compliments, Robson's then assistant let something slip out that would remain in Faria's memory: "Take a coaching course and one day you might even come and work with me."

Two years later the promise was fulfilled. Rui Faria was a high school teacher when the phone rang one afternoon: "What's your availability to come and work with me?" asked Mourinho. The young teacher couldn't believe it. "If it was up to me I'd already have started yesterday! Just tell me when and where, and I'll go", Faria replied.

The following decade shaped the professional side of Rui Faria. This assistant is the most genuine example of someone José Mourinho formatted from head to toe, as he himself admits: "Obviously I had knowledge and value, I had potential, but to me it was all new. He already had a wealth of experience and then he kept exerting his influence on me, every day. That's one of his strongest features: shaping those who work for him, so as to carry out his ideas and his objectives."

A FOCUS ON VICTORY

24th January, 2010. At half-time, the Cup game between Inter and Milan was at 1-0, to Inter, after a very complicated first half: Sneijder was expelled and Lúcio got a very strained yellow card. The referee, namely Mr. Rocchi, was totally against Inter.

I decided to go to the changing rooms, which is something I don't usually do. But that day I went, because I was afraid there would be too much nervous tension caused by the circumstances and by the referee's behaviour.

I opened the door and... surprise, surprise! Instead of feeling nervous tension or hearing complaints about the referee, caused by everything that had happened on the pitch, I listened to an incredible, almost unreal silence. Almost on tiptoe I crossed the corridor to see what was going on in the room where the players were with Mourinho. He was

standing up at the centre and the players were sitting in their places, calm like anything. While drawing on a blackboard, Mourinho was explaining tactics for the second half, saying their posture shouldn't change and that, despite being outnumbered, he wouldn't admit fear or anxiety vis-a-vis the opponent. Insisting on the moves some of the players should do, Mourinho stressed the greater effort they would have to make, as a consequence of the team playing with ten men: "They're going to get nervous, because they're not going to manage to score against ten, and we seize the opportunity, score another goal and win."

The game finished at 2-0, as he had predicted. The referee still had time to expel Lúcio almost at the end of the match, with a second yellow, and we played 5 more minutes with 9 players.

What impressed me the most in this story was Mourinho's capacity at half-time. Without saying a word about the controversies of the first *half or the referee's actions, he preferred to talk about the game and the way the athletes should behave to win, which in fact happened. He took a positive stance, instead of emphasising the negative aspects.*

I have to say, this exceptional episode made my esteem for José Mourinho soar. A coach always focused on results, passionately going for the win."

MASSIMO MORATTI

THE AMBITIOUS ONE...

Mourinho manages to convince everyone that no objective is unattainable.

AITOR KARANKA

Mourinho makes us have more character and be more ambitious.

IKER CASILLAS

mbition – is this a cursed word or a concept of virtues? Ambition, like Ambient, comes from the Latin 'ambire', that is, 'to move freely'. A literal translation of Ambition, and in this case the best of all, would mean creating one's own path. It's knowing what you want out of life and trying to get there. Not everyone can take their destiny into their own hands.

José Mourinho can. He often leaves his comfort zone, takes risks and constantly puts his limits to the test. He walks his path without accepting impositions.

Mourinho doesn't lose his capacity to strive for more and more, even though he's already won so much. "The motivation with which he faces each project is unusual. Even after three hundred or so victories, his desire to win is the same as it was the very first time", confesses Rui Faria, his closest assistant.

Deco was also amazed by Mourinho's constant desire to want more and more: "The secret, in my opinion, is that although he knows he's very good he stays humble, he continues to work hard to be able to win more."

Despite being number one in the World, he continues to work more than the others. **DECO**

The Luso-Brazilian Deco, considered essential in FC Porto's strategy as winner of the UEFA Cup in 2003 and European champion in 2004, guarantees that José Mourinho was always the first to show frustration and the players followed in his footsteps: "No matter how good he is, he knows he can't rest on his laurels because there's always someone keen to occupy the throne. I've always admired him for that."

FC Porto was probably the club where José Mourinho's ambition sounded more out of place. His rhetoric, filled with big promises, sounded like a madman's talk, when compared to the recent, depressing past of the club. Often Mourinho seemed to produce monologues that only he believed in. Him, and as it eventually turned out, the players.

Athletes such as Costinha recall a time when the capacity to strive for more came to be crucial for attaining success: "At the time Mourinho was unknown. As were many of us too. It's obvious we were good players, but far from being able to dream of European titles. Maybe we could win the national championship, but nothing more. And he managed to convince us it was possible. He awakened our self-confidence, the capacity we had, but weren't able to show. Without him we wouldn't have been European champions."

Jorge Costa, the captain of Mourinho's victories in FC Porto, remembers the beginning of a journey that had everything to go wrong... but it turned out well: "That year, in 2002, when I came from England on his request, I started seeing new players being recruited and I felt wary. There were players coming from União de Leiria, from Vitória de Setúbal, players I knew but about whom I honestly had some misgivings.

I must admit I thought it would be difficult to fight for the championship." Jorge Costa gradually changed his mind as the training period in France moved on. The training methods were innovative and the team spirit unbreakable. But the real lever was ambition.

He's dissatisfied by nature; he doesn't hold onto success, he's in constant evolution, always wanting more for himself. **JORGE COSTA**

If anyone doubts José Mourinho's unquenchable thirst, he himself confirms it with a bold example: "When I won the award for best coach in the world, I remember having said: to win the next game is more important than this. I still think exactly the same way. And I think the players should also think that way. More important than winning an individual trophy is winning the next game. I'd never swap a victory in the next game for any individual award."

Individual trophies are a mere consequence of something Mourinho won't swap for anything: the team's victories, the titles. Those are at the heart of his ambition. "To me there wasn't much of a difference between the three times I was elected the best, the time I was elected second best and the time I was elected third best. I think being among the best is what's truly meaningful. Then winning or not winning is something more subjective. It depends a little on people's tastes. Anyway, no-one can be the best every time."

AMBITIOUS OR ARROGANT?

The adjective ambitious is often mistaken for arrogant. Mourinho knows that only too well. The Portuguese coach's interventions are almost always interpreted this way. Like his answer to the question we asked him for this book: What's your strongest point as a coach? "Perhaps my answer is going to provide further arguments to those

critics who like to call me arrogant, vain and conceited. But what can I say?"

I consider myself to be a great coach, I consider myself to be a complete coach, I consider myself to be a strong coach in almost every respect. I don't really have many weaknesses in the areas that make a football coach these days. So I think I'm a very balanced coach. To me, it's difficult to talk about one quality being superior to another. **JOSÉ MOURINHO**

José Mourinho definitely rejects the public humility that is so popular in the public eye. Self-confidence is not strategic. Expressions of ambition are not rhetoric. Mourinho strongly believes what he says. And these seemingly unconscious traits are what allows him to face each and every challenge – more or less difficult – in the same manner. "Before any important game, the coach is obviously nervous and concerned. With him the opposite happens", says Jorge Mendes. "The ease he shows before difficult games is astounding. You've got to be close to him to know. He's confident and he passes that confidence to the players", the entrepreneur concludes.

These features come from long ago, from when the now twice European champion was just an assistant: "When he was van Gaal's assistant in Barcelona, I remember an ambitious young man, who lived and breathed football and wanted to learn in order to advance", Vítor Baía points out. Only later did it become clear: Mourinho was an assistant, but he hid a huge capacity to absorb knowledge. He wasn't a mere assistant; in fact there was nothing simple about him. He looked at the future as an ever-increasing challenge, never in a static perspective.

His first experience as leader, with Benfica, confirmed what everybody suspected: Mourinho had an unusual dose of ambition and revealed a total lack of fear in the face of obstacles. And, above all, he passed on this message to the players in an incisive and effective manner. Maniche tells us what used to happen when he was coached by Mourinho in FC Porto: "It was already a habit. On the way to Lisbon, all of us, players, coaches and staff, would bet by how many goals we'd beat Benfica or Sporting. Whoever lost had to pay for lunch. We'd bet because we knew we'd win."

Over time the Portuguese coach built up an image of a wizard, capable of shaping destiny with his own hands. "Many times we thought he was a sorcerer because in most situations, perhaps 95% of them, he'd guess what would happen on the pitch", explains Maniche. The succession of such episodes ranked Mourinho high among the players. The message spread. No-one dared dispute the leader's words, everyone shared the same ambition, as remote as it might seem.

And this was how a group of basically unknown players won the UEFA Cup and the Champions League in two consecutive years, for FC Porto. Maniche provides an illustrative example: "In the Euro 2004, when everyone thought we were going to win the final, we lost. I'm sure that, if Mourinho had been the national coach, that victory would've been ours."

This former FC Porto midfielder, who would later play again with Mourinho for Chelsea, further explains: "It would've started right outside the Alcochete Academy, where we'd have been in the training course. He'd never have allowed the players to have to deal with that euphoria that grew around the National Team. He'd run away from the fans and protect the players. That's what he did in the finals of the Champions League and of the UEFA Cup. He was totally thorough in the preparation of the team. For one simple reason: he knows the finals are to win. And often you only get one chance in life."

AMBITION IN SEVERAL LANGUAGES

Mourinho loves to win. Who doesn't? But in Mourinho's case this desire is at the top of the list and the remaining items are just accessories to achieve victory. Winning is an obsession in his head: "He doesn't know how to lose and he doesn't like to lose in any way", assures assistant Rui Faria. That's why, for him, there is no such thing as insurmountable obstacles to begin with.

That's how it was when he got to Chelsea in 2004. In a country where tradition is law (even in football), José Mourinho changed the paradigm of competition, as Peter Kenyon, then sports director of the London club, recalls:

He arrived and right in the first season he dynamited the dominance of two Goliaths (Manchester United and Arsenal) of the League that many people believe to be the best of the world. He got here and changed that dominance forever. That's fantastic. **PETER KENYON**

Didier Drogba was one of the essential players used by Mourinho in the transformation of Chelsea. This Ivory Coast player will never forget the unique, magical talk of the genius:

He loves winning. Most coaches get to a club and say: "I'm going to try and win, it's going to be hard..." He says: "I'm here to win", and he wins. That makes him special. **DIDIER DROGBA**

The 'injections' of motivation touched the soul of the Blues and transformed a group of good athletes into a team capable of beating the best. "Before he arrived we had good players: John Terry, Frank Lampard... they were quality players, without a doubt", says Drogba. "Take me: when I got here I already knew how to play football. Petr Cech, he also knew how to play football. But José transformed good players into winning players. Even after Mourinho left, that state of mind remained. He left that legacy to Chelsea."

Mourinho's 'brand' stayed in London. Perhaps forever. Mourinho left, in search of new challenges, because of an incentive called 'ambition'.

He landed in Milan and found a club with a different historical background. Before Mourinho, Inter could already flaunt 17 Italian championships, two Champions Leagues and three UEFA Cups, among its extensive list of trophies. Inter was already a European giant, totally different from Chelsea. The art of the Portuguese coach was to discover new stimuli capable of fulfilling the players, encouraging the fans and quenching their own ambition. He found one, essential stimulus, and pursued it passionately: the European Championship.

When Inter had won the trophy for the last time, this competition was still called European Champions Clubs' Cup. Winning it again would be... huge. And for Mourinho there was an extra 'carrot', as he himself explains: "Entering that stadium (Santiago Bernabéu) and knowing I could go down in history as one of the few coaches who won the Champions for two different clubs, was tremendously meaningful to me."

Capitão Zanetti, who for 16 years had witnessed the parade of coaches in the club, understood the differences immediately: "From the start we saw that a very capable, very intelligent coach had arrived, with great character and great professionalism. That was very good for the team and helped us accomplish what we accomplished." And Inter Milan won the Champions League again, 45 years later.

It's this capacity to form groups and put them on the track to victory, always reflecting different objectives, that makes Mourinho stand out. He doesn't just win in that one club, in that one country, with that specific group of players or in that given sport context. Mourinho wins because he himself assimilates that intense desire and moves those around him to assimilate it as well. That's why there's no better way to sum it up better than Rui Faria does:

Science brought us cloning, but cloning him is impossible, because beyond the biological factors, there's experience and recognition, built over time, which allow him to be different, impossible to be copied. **RUI FARIA**

A YOUNG MAN OF VALUE WHO WENT FAR

I first met José Mourinho when Bobby Robson was Porto's coach. He was his assistant but he gained notoriety and prestige in that technical team. He had great influence over Bobby Robson who, despite being very experienced, had a lot of faith in Mourinho's opinions. Robson always told me: "This guy's really valuable… he's going places." Such ambition in someone still so young really impressed me.

At that time we created great empathy, even friendship, for each other. The night Bobby Robson went to my house to say he had received an invitation from Barcelona and wanted to leave FC Porto, my admiration for Mourinho grew even stronger. The process wasn't easy – there were deep divergences with Bobby Robson and even with Barcelona – and yet Mourinho was just perfect. He always said the truth and was overly correct. My admiration for him grew all the more.

I kept a close watch on his career. When he left Benfica, whenever I talked to club presidents I always mentioned that Mourinho would be a very successful coach. I even suggested him to some managers. I remember one of the presidents who consulted me was João Bartolomeu, from União de Leiria, with whom I often spoke about football.

When I told him about José Mourinho's qualities, he just asked me: "But do you think Mourinho can coach FC Porto?" I said: "I haven't the slightest doubt. The only reason he's not going to FC Porto right away is because he's got to go to another club first, but he sure will be coach for FC Porto." In view of this, Bartolomeu answered: "If he's good enough for FC Porto then he's good enough for Leiria." And he hired him.

Later on, another funny episode happened, once again revealing Mourinho's ambition. In a conversation with João Bartolomeu, he confided: "President, I'm in trouble! The man's crazy, all he wants is to attack, he thinks this is FC Porto." I replied: "Hold it, you know how to manage Leiria and that's already a miracle. He knows about football. Let him attack. And if he wants to play with 11 strikers, stay out of it." A few months later he admitted that José Mourinho really was amazing. And he was. He built his career as he did in Leiria with an average team.

At the time, in the 2001/02 season, FC Porto was going through a bad phase. There was a lack of belief because of the bad results. One day I get a call from Baidek, the businessman, asking if I believed in Mourinho as coach. I said yes and reminded him that I'd been the one to suggest him to União de Leiria. Baidek replied: "Well let me tell you then that Mourinho's going to be presented on the 29th of December as coach of Benfica." I started adding things up in my mind and asked out loud: "But how are they going to present him only on the 29th if today is still the 22nd?" Baidek explained: "Well, Veiga's spending Christmas in Luxemburg and he makes a point of being here at the presentation."

It was all I needed to hear. I asked Baidek to set up a meeting immediately with José Mourinho. FC Porto had a coach, Octávio Machado, and it was my intention to keep him until the end of the season, but then…

João Bartolomeu was already suspecting of Benfica's interest and he called me. I told him that FC Porto might also be interested but that he would be informed if this went forward.

On 27th December I spoke with Baidek again. We set a meeting for the following day, the 28th – at my place – precisely on the eve of the presentation in Benfica and also my birthday.

It was funny because that day I had some people over for my birthday party. I settled with Baidek that we'd meet after dinner. They'd wait outside until the living room lights went out. That was the signal to show that my guests had already left.

I remember several people were there and around midnight I began to say I was tired, I had a headache, I was sleepy… to see if they would go away. It worked. Around one in the morning I had no-one at home. Baidek walked in with Mourinho and Baltemar Brito.

We started talking at three in the morning and reached the following deal: Mourinho would stay put in Leiria until the end of the season and only then, when Octávio left FC Porto, would he become our coach. I called Mr. Caldeira, who was already sleeping, to come over with the contract ready to be signed.

Meanwhile things in FC Porto took a turn for the worse. The atmosphere became unbearable and Octávio ran out of space to go on. At that point I contacted Mourinho again and told him that after all it wasn't to be at the end of the season, it was right now.

Mourinho did the absolute right thing. He asked me to first solve things with Octávio, because he didn't want to give rise to any problems. So that's what happened. We reached a deal with Octávio and only after that did I have lunch with João Bartolomeu in Mealhada to reach an understanding for him to release Mourinho to us halfway through the contract.

Right away, at the presentation to the players, in the changing room, something important happened, showing Mourinho's ambition, once again: he said to the players, with the utmost confidence, "next year we are going to be the champions!" The very same sentence he would repeat a few minutes later at the press conference. There and then, he revealed his common sense, conviction and confidence in the future. It reminded me of that phrase of Bobby Robson five years earlier: "This guy's really valuable… he's going places." Everyone knows the rest of the story.

JORGE NUNO PINTO DA COSTA

Que o futuro lhe traga a continuação dos sucessos, que tem merece, são os meus votos ao amigo José Mourinho.

That the future may bring you a lot of success, which you certainly deserve, is what I wish to my friend José Mourinho.

Dedication by Pinto da Costa

CHARISMA…

I have a special connection with Mourinho, it's hard to explain. Despite being a substitute, he made me a better player, and I am grateful to him for that. He's a coach who makes the most of his players and makes them better.

ESTEBAN GRANERO

Just like all the others, I'm really proud of having been a part of your history. It was an important time in my career. Keep it up! See you soon.

DIDIER DROGBA

José Mourinho is a social magnet. He attracts players, fans, journalists, sponsors and even those for whom football is not at the top of their priority list. This phenomenon of attraction, influence and fascination is called charisma.

The Catechism Compendium of the Catholic Church provides rather a less prosaic definition: charismas "are special gifts of the Holy Spirit, bestowed upon someone for the good of men, for the needs of the world and, especially, for the edification of the Church." Taken literally, this could mean that José Mourinho might be risen, and rightly so, to a godlike state. A God of football.

These are slippery grounds, on which we should tread carefully. So let's stick to the simpler definition. Charisma is related to the way a person is and acts. The way Mourinho is and acts leaves a trail, a longing and even tears. It was like this in all the places where he passed and with everyone he was in touch with.

What is it that makes players follow José Mourinho 'to the death'? It can't be explained rationally. Jorge Costa, who was one of the captains on Mourinho's team (in FC Porto), has no explanation:

What I'd really like to be able to justify is the willingness the players have, and that I also had, to follow him 'to the death'. **JORGE COSTA**

The current coach of Cluj goes on: "I'd also like to know, because I myself am a coach and I'd also like my group to follow me 'to the death'. I've no idea what the formula is and probably he doesn't know it himself. Actually, I don't even think there is a formula, things just happen naturally. Not even Mourinho himself can explain in a simple, natural manner how it's possible to have a group of players equally united in the good and the bad moments. And in that group there are only 11 who are playing, because the other seven go to the bench and another six or seven don't even get equipped."

Petr Cech can't explain the magnetism of the Portuguese coach. He just admits to a contagious pleasure in their relationship, starting with the training sessions: "It was always a pleasure to come to work. When you have that special atmosphere and you work with the people you really care about, you enjoy everything and you miss them when they leave. He was a special character and you just never forget that kind of person."

José Mourinho's persuasive skill is so obvious that even those who follow him from afar can sense it. Florentino Pérez doesn't have daily contact with Mourinho, but he's already identified this incredible capacity to draw the whole world, even when that world is called Real Madrid: "I'm totally convinced that we're on the right track. What I'm seeing now I hadn't seen in a long time: a group of players and coaches with a perfect empathy, dream and professionalism, with will power and a spirit of sacrifice for a common cause."

The Merengue president has no doubt José Mourinho and Real Madrid are a perfect fit: "Besides being a great professional and leader, I find the respect he has for the values of this centuries-old institution remarkable. The best club in the world of the 20th century – elected by FIFA – was in need of a coach to go with this title, and now it has one. I believe they complement each other perfectly, like a motor and a car. They were made for each other."

FROM ONE GENIUS TO ANOTHER

Jorge Mendes, arguably one of the men who knows José Mourinho best, doesn't hesitate to declare that the Portuguese coach is among the best ever: "He did a remarkable job for the teams he coached. It's really hard to find someone with his capacity, he's a genius! In the next 500 years it's going to be difficult to find someone like him." The entrepreneur, whose occupation is precisely to find exceptional players and coaches, knows what he's talking about. "If he were to stop coaching tomorrow, he'd probably go down in history as the best coach ever, not just of football but of sports in general. What he's done so far is unreal." In Jorge Mendes' opinion, José Mourinho's genius, strongly sustained by his charisma, even goes beyond frontiers of sports. "With this leadership capacity, he'd make it in any area of society, I'm sure."

The words genius and charisma are also perfect for another football figure: Diego Armando Maradona. But even this charismatic, supreme genius bows to Mourinho's skills.

Mourinho has what a coach most desires: the players' respect. I've talked to players from Chelsea, from Inter, from Porto and even from Real Madrid, and no-one has a bad word to say about him. They all show respect and admiration, which is very difficult to conquer in football. **DIEGO MARADONA**

El Pibe also adds: "It's not easy to be in charge of a group. In football it's always a problem when you pick one player instead of another. For Mourinho that was never a problem or, if it was, it stayed behind closed doors, which is decisive for winning the group's trust."

Maradona and Mourinho have never worked together. They met during a visit the Argentine paid to the Inter Milan training centre. When they first met, Maradona realised straight away what a special person he had before him: "It was as if we'd known each other for 15 years. He treated me wonderfully." There was immediate empathy. Mourinho was one of millions who delighted in Maradona's dribbles as a player. He never thought he'd win the respect of his all-time idol. The truth is that after this first contact at the Inter training centre, their friendship became huge. While preparing for the 2010 World Championship, Diego Maradona – then the national coach of the Pampas – often asked Mourinho for advice on the best choices to make. The Portuguese coach would always help him, and gladly. Today, Maradona and Mourinho are friends for life.

The world had proof of that when, in January 2011, Maradona paid a surprise visit to the Real Madrid sports city. That day, Mourinho didn't want to say goodbye to the genius without offering him an autographed Real Madrid shirt. The dedication says it all: "I am embarrassed to sign a shirt for Don Diego. You are World's number one. I love you."

All this places Maradona in the best position to qualify Mourinho's charisma. Don Diego, as the Portuguese coach calls him, discovered a different shine in Mourinho's eyes the moment they met: "I saw his eyes had that light of someone who's very dear to the players. Zanetti had already told me about this, but seeing it myself was different." El Pibe feels that the personality Mourinho gave the Real Madrid team in such a short time is the best example of his charismatic capacity: "Real Madrid has long been buying and buying and buying... they had the best players but didn't play well or win as many times as they should. That club was a mess. Mourinho changed everything. In a short time he gave the team identity and shape. That's really difficult in a club like Real Madrid. Much, much harder than in Barcelona, for instance, because Guardiola is Catalan and the identity is already there. What Mourinho transmits is called charisma and personality."

This capacity, or gift, to have an impact, at first sight, on even the least impressionable, like Maradona, keeps happening in José Mourinho's professional life. Peter Kenyon, former chief executive of Chelsea, recalls an illustrative episode that took place in 2004, when Mourinho began talks that would eventually take him to the London club:

Roman (Abramovich) and I flew on purpose to a European city, for our first meeting with José, at which Jorge Mendes was also present. It was a hugely important meeting. But due to obligations he couldn't postpone, José was two and a half hours late. And we waited two and a half hours for him! The meeting might very well not have taken place. But it did, and everything worked out because in five minutes it was clear he was the right man for the job. **PETER KENYON**

The former strongman of Chelsea went on: "It was quite visible that he thought in a different way, that his methods were progressive. He practically represented a new breed of coaches, very technical, very methodical. We immediately felt he was the perfect catalyst to catapult Chelsea on to the path of success." That day, in Vigo, Jorge Mendes ordered a table full of seafood to mark the solemnity of the moment. Abramovich ate a lettuce leaf.

Peter Kenyon wasn't mistaken. José Mourinho transformed Chelsea into a top club and his charisma turned out to be decisive right in the first few weeks. "He had two very important achievements in the initial phase: transforming the excellent players Chelsea had, but who had never won anything, into winning players; and attracting other athletes to the club by using his skill and personality to convince them of what could happen in the future."

Mourinho's charisma often collided head on with Abramovich's equally strong personality. The Russian millionaire was not always capable of believing in the Portuguese coach's far-reaching vision. Peter Kenyon was a privileged witness of this duel. "There were moments of tension, it's true, because they're both very passionate characters in their respective jobs, but I can guarantee they had an enormous respect for each other. Roman supported Chelsea's development, the funding of acquisitions, José's decisions one hundred per cent... but I'm sure he only did it because he had confidence in his competence and in his charisma."

José Mourinho and Alex Ferguson are two of the best living examples of success when it comes to managing teams. Peter Kenyon was lucky enough to work with both. Despite their different paths, there are obvious similarities between them, mostly based on charisma and personality: "The way Ferguson successively built competitive teams over 25 years in Manchester United is remarkable, as is the success Mourinho had in three different countries, environments and cultures. Although they have big differences in style, they also have many similarities in substance. Both are absolute winners and that shows in everything they do."

SAUDADE (LONGING) IN EVERY LANGUAGE

Frank Lampard was injured when he heard the news that Mourinho was saying goodbye to Chelsea. Despite having already heard rumours, the England international admits he felt an unusual sadness that day: "In my mind I'd imagined he was going to stay for 10 years. Everything worked perfectly. The moment he said goodbye to us was really very sad. Normally I don't get emotionally involved in this kind of thing. I know coaches come and go. But in this case it was more than a coach leaving, it was a friend leaving us. It was a hard day for me."

It was a hard day for the whole of the Chelsea team. No-one could accept the news. John Terry, the captain, took charge and tried the impossible:

When I learned he was leaving, around midnight, I called Didier and Frank and I told them: "We can't allow this!" We spoke with the club and clearly told them we didn't want him to go. But José already had a deal to leave. **JOHN TERRY**

The captain is sure that "everyone in Chelsea, and not just the players, but all the staff, have José Mourinho in their hearts."

The word is typically Portuguese, but Lampard doesn't shy away from using it as a faithful translation of a common feeling that lingers to this day at Stamford Bridge: "Yes, I feel saudades. I've been very lucky with the coaches I've worked with throughout my career, but Mourinho will always have a special place in my heart. My best years were with him and in that regard I feel saudades. I'm sure many of the people here will say the same."

And in this case it's reasonable to say that the feeling is shared by everyone, from the president to the groundsman. Literally. In the 2004/05 pre-season, when Mourinho got to Chelsea, the club won a tournament in the United States, whose main attraction happened to be 'just' the new European champion AC Milan. José Mourinho surprised everyone by dedicating the victory and the trophy to... the Chelsea groundsman. He explained that was the deserved award for someone who had taken such wonderful care of the Stamford Bridge pitch, where Chelsea had been training for 30 days before travelling to the States. Mourinho not only won a friend -- transformed into star of the company for several days by the English press – but he won the respect of the whole club. From top to bottom.

This mysterious capacity to fascinate is so deep it leaves its roots behind. It was already strange enough to hear a full stadium chanting the name of a coach, and this happened with every club José Mourinho was in. One of the most breathtaking episodes happened in 2005, at Stamford Bridge, during a match against Seville for the Champions League. The Blues were already winning 4-0 and the delirious crowd spontaneously began to chant: "Stand up, stand up for the Special One", at the same time as the whole stadium bowed in the direction of the Portuguese coach.

But hearing those chants long after Mourinho left would seem impossible. And yet it happened. "It's amazing how the fans kept chanting his name many months after he'd left", says Drogba, "for us, players, it's a pleasure. It feels good to hear his name shouted by the fans. It's proof that he's part and parcel of the history of the club, and that's that. He's there, he left his print and it will last forever."

To this day, almost three years later, Peter Kenyon hasn't come to terms with the separation. It was the best time of Chelsea's history and the best professional experience of the former chief executive. "It was still the start of our project, not the end. I was disappointed that I, José and Chelsea itself weren't able to create the conditions to work longer. I'm sure we would have been even more successful. Besides, when he left I was the one who had to pick up the pieces and I can tell you it was hard work."

José Mourinho's departure was not just a problem for Chelsea – it represented an irreparable loss to the Premier League.

"His passage through our championship was a very happy time for English football. Even players and fans from other clubs, even the average citizen, everyone acknowledges that José had that ability to attract people to football. He made a very valuable contribution to English football", Peter Kenyon points out.

The reflection of this feeling described by Peter Kenyon was more visible on the day Mourinho left. Didier Drogba was impressed with the unusual demonstrations of the English media:

When he left England I saw television reports identical to those they do when someone famous dies. Amazing! The English realised they were going to lose a huge personality, a gentleman of football and of that championship. It was an enormous show of respect. **DIDIER DROGBA**

That's why the post-Mourinho era is miserable for any club. The season following José Mourinho's departure, FC Porto, the European and Portuguese champion and Portugal Cup finalist, went no further than the Champions' eighth-finals, the second place in the championship and nowhere near the Cup final. Five years passed and Chelsea, twice English champion with Mourinho, had to wait three years to reconquer the title and has already switched coach four times. The great Inter, overall winner of the trophies with the Portuguese coach in 2009/10, lost two cups in a row the following season, with Rafa Benítez in charge, and has swapped coach another three times in little more than a year (Leonardo, Gasperini and now Ranieri).

As time goes by, demonstrations of how much Mourinho is missed arise from the least expected places, as is the case, for instance, of Josep Lluis Nuñez, Barcelona's former historical president who, in a recent statement to Catalonia Radio, said: "I have fond memories of Mourinho, he's a wonderful person. It was a mistake to let him go, when he triumphed in Barcelona. We won two leagues with him as van Gaal's assistant and the following year, when he wasn't around anymore, we weren't champions." Nuñez's words fell like a bomb in Catalonia. Here was the president of Barcelona for 22 years – having won over 30 titles in football alone – praising the current coach of his eternal, visceral rival regarding his time in Barcelona just as an assistant, after 11 years.

'MOURINHO STYLE'

The clothes he wears, the knot of his tie and the unruly stubble are image traits that also contribute to the construction of charismatic Mourinho.

Simple habits or innocent gestures assume enormous proportions in the body of the Portuguese coach. An emblematic example happened in England with the famous grey Armani overcoat. In his first year in Chelsea, the London cold forced Mourinho to choose suitable clothing. He went for the overcoat – subtly used with the collar up, Cantona-style – and he never let go of it again during all the games. As the victories came rolling in, superstitious interpretations regarding the overcoat multiplied. A simple item of clothing, used millions of times by hundreds of other coaches in England, was becoming a cult object on José Mourinho's body. In such a way that Mourinho's Chelsea hadn't even ended the first season and already the champion coach's overcoat – with his name embroidered on the collar – was being auctioned on the internet with revenues going to CLIC Sargent, an institution for cancer-stricken children, of which Mourinho was patron. He actually made a bid himself for 15 thousand pounds and Jorge Mendes raised it to 20 thousand, but someone offered more and kept the overcoat. Later on, Chelsea tried to recover it – to give it a prominent place in the Museum – and, in an act of goodwill, the person who had bought it ended up donating it to the club.

But the odyssey concerning José Mourinho's overcoat doesn't end here. Around the same time someone had the idea of making T-shirts with the image of the famous coat. Later the same object became… a work of art. The Portuguese sculptor José Coelho created a piece called 'Soul-Overcoat', based on the coach's attire. The sculpture earned the artist national and international projection.

It was a time of total madness surrounding José Mourinho. Chelsea fans worshipped him just as someone would bow down to a God.

For the game that gave them the title, in the 2005/06 season, Mourinho no longer wore the overcoat, dressing simply in a black coat and tie, with a Portugal scarf around his neck. That spring afternoon, under a rare London sun, Chelsea only needed a tie, but it thrashed arch-rival Manchester United with a solid 3-0. Mourinho thus gained the second English title at the helm of Chelsea. The crowd was delirious, shouting out his name. After receiving the two medals of victory, the coach approached the Blues 'hardcore' fans and threw the medals towards them. Then he took off his coat and threw it also to the same fans, thus paying a warm tribute to those who had acclaimed him.

Two years later one of the medals ended up in the shop window of Bonham, the famous Chester auction house, and, to the sound of auctioneer Dan Davies' gavel, it was bought by a stranger for 30 thousand Euros. As for the black coat, it was sold on eBay for over 200 thousand Euros.

The Mourinho brand is always profound, whether it concerns the titles he wins, or a simple overcoat. So profound, in fact, that in 2010 – three years after the Portuguese coach had left Chelsea -, Carlo Ancelotti felt obliged to comment on Mourinho's omnipresence in the club through his… overcoat: "I know very well what he gave to Chelsea, he even left his overcoat here."

Today, the 'Mourinho style' is a well-defined concept that breeds passions and has more and more fans. It is precisely that style that attracts the world's leading brands, anxious to 'become one' with José Mourinho's winning image. His immediate success, reached right after he moved to England, aroused the interest of several companies that tried to reproduce his working methods.

Publicity carried José Mourinho's charisma beyond the boundaries of football. The big bang happened in 2005, through Samsung, which filled the world with billboards showing the coach's face. Mourinho surrendered to the facts: "This is it. There's no turning back. I think any old lady, even one who doesn't like football, will recognise me."

Time only spread the phenomenon. He's the only football coach with popularity levels identical to, or even higher than, the best players in the world. In a recent interview to the Turkish newspaper Hürriyet, José Mourinho himself explained to what extent this popularity helps in managing star-filled groups: "They view themselves as football icons, but they look at me and they also see an icon. They see me as one of them. It's not easy to run a team of this calibre unless you're an icon. Between them and me, there's no difference of status."

The popularity gave rise to a cult. Today, José Mourinho is universally and transversally present in society.

A CHARISMATIC GUY

I met José Mourinho in 2007, at the traditional UEFA Champions League meeting of coaches, in Nyon. He was coaching Chelsea, I was with Fenerbahçe. It was a very pleasant meeting, we instantly got on well. Mourinho admitted to being my fan, from the time I was in Flamengo, and that he'd even had photos of me up on his bedroom walls. He joked about sadly never having been much of a player himself, so he had all the more appreciation for the stars of that time.

I already had a very good impression of José Mourinho. Everyone spoke well about him, namely Carlos Mozer, who played with me for many years and was his assistant at the start of his career. But during that meeting in Nyon I became totally convinced he was really special. I realised there were two 'Mourinhos': the relentless, hard one, who presented himself to the media; and the other one, a friendly guy open to dialogue in his personal relationships.

During that meeting, I also became aware of his charisma. I understood better why, wherever Mourinho goes, the group always follows him. Kezman, a Serbian player who was coached by him in Chelsea and then was with me in Fernerbahçe, had already talked to me about this. Mourinho's a guy open to dialogue, that's for sure. He's a guy who transmits confidence and encourages team unity, quite effortlessly. Quite effortlessly precisely because his charisma has already done half the work.

Charisma is an essential feature in a leader. I can say that from my own experience. Charisma demands respect, justice, discipline and many other factors that are essential to relationships within a working group. A charismatic leader can explain in a better and easier way to those under his command the benefits of complying with the rules.

As a coach, I also feel that nowadays. Curiously, in my early days as coach, it wasn't quite like that. There were times when my charisma, conquered during my career as a player, even got in the way. Let me explain this better: often I felt that my athletes had more respect for the charisma of the idol (player), than for the authority of the coach. That was very clear in Fenerbahçe, where there were top athletes who remembered my football career very well. Fortunately I managed to reverse that fact and the problem no longer exists. Mourinho doesn't run that risk. His charisma was built on victories and on the unique way he has connected with the different groups, always as coach.

The Nyon meeting was the first and only one I had with José Mourinho, so far. In the meantime we've always talked through intermediaries, such as goalkeeper Júlio César, when Mourinho was coaching Inter Milan, through whom I'd always send "a hug to the boss."

Despite the distance between us, a mutual appreciation has always remained, and even some identification in terms of values. I wish José the best of luck – because talent he's already got in abundance – and I hope to be with him one day for longer – maybe in a club he runs -, to understand even better his methods and the reason for his charisma.

ZICO

DISCIPLINE...

Everything Mourinho did was for my own good and for the good of the group. I didn't mind the statements he made. I know him and I know that when he wants someone to give it his all he says things like that.

PEDRO LEÓN

Sometimes we're in the tunnel and he says if we're going to play well or not and if we're going to suffer a goal... I don't know what kind of gift he has, but it's hallucinating!

KARIM BENZEMA

Maniche, Vítor Baía, Costinha, Carlos Alberto, Ricardo Carvalho, Balotelli, Eto´o, Pedro Léon… it's a long list. And it will be never-ending as long as José Mourinho coaches football teams.

These players know the tight grip of his rules. They are the protagonists of tough scenes, almost all of them played out in public, and most of them solved by the coach with no mercy. The stories have one point in common: despite the severity applied by José Mourinho in every case, the players always acknowledged their own fault and gave reason to the coach. In some cases the targeted players even thanked him profusely for the valuable lessons they learned.

The first difficult case in José Mourinho's career happened at the end of 2000, at the service of Benfica. With only a few months' leadership, the coach decided to play a practice match between the red club's main team and its B team. Mourinho chose to watch the game from the crowd's stand and he asked Carlos Mozer – then assistant coach – to sit on the bench. They were to call each other if any relevant incident so required.

The match was still in the first part when young Diogo Luís (left-back for the B team) steals the ball from Maniche (then one of the most hopeful players of Benfica), and he goes to half-time playing really well. Clearly offended with the 'cheek', Maniche goes after Diogo Luís and hits him from behind, with a kick, and no ball to battle for. One second later Mozer's mobile phone rings at the bench: "Make that (…) run until the end of the game!" ordered Mourinho. His assistant complied: "I called Maniche and informed him of this decision. His immediate reply was 'I'm not going!' I warned him it was best to obey the order because the coach was a new one, with a different attitude from the others and if he said so you just did it." After 10 minutes, visibly displeased, Maniche finally started running. He took 45 long minutes to go round the green twice. Mourinho saw this, jotted it down and went back to it the following day.

In the morning, he called Carlos Mozer and Ángel Vilda (the physical trainer) to inform them that from that moment on Maniche would be training at a different time from the other colleagues. Later, before the whole team and Maniche himself, he said: "Maniche is doing very poorly physically." The player quivered and reacted immediately: "No I'm not, Mister!" Mourinho explained, in a calm tone of voice: "Yes, you are. A player who runs twice around the field in 45 minutes can't play, he's really unwell physically, and so from today onwards you're going to train at midday with Mozer and Vilda until you get back to shape and can return to the group."

The leader's words echoed in the training field. In the background, only the players' breathing was heard. His head hanging down, Maniche didn't fight back either. Minutes later, in private, he approached assistant coach Mozer to underline his point: "Mozer, I'm fine physically!"

The former centre-back's answer silenced Maniche: "I warned you things aren't as they used to be, they've changed now…"

Maniche trained all week alone with the two assistants. He trained well. He trained like he'd never trained before. Punctual, hard-working and determined. Mozer reported this to José Mourinho at the end of the week: "His behaviour was exemplary." Despite his effort, Maniche wasn't called for the weekend meet. He returned to the group the following week – no smiles but working hard. Another weekend, another call. Maniche's name was there. What's more, as captain of the team. The midfielder found this odd and approached Mozer, once again to rant: "Come and see this, Mozer, I think he's got it wrong! He put as me captain? Go talk to him, there must be a mistake." Mozer couldn't resist telling the boss about this episode. So then Mourinho asked Maniche to come over and gave him a truly biblical sermon: the importance of being the only player in the team trained in the club's youth system, the responsibility of setting the example for the younger ones, the obligation to be the last one to leave the boat: these words revolutionised Maniche's head. "The one player everyone described as crazy and unstable, became an unstoppable competitive machine", says Mozer.

Eleven years on, Maniche recalls this episode with respect and salutes the coach's gesture:

He helped me take responsibility. That punishment made me think and changed my way of being. These are the details great men and great players are made of. He helped me be more grown up in a lot of things, that was just the first episode. He made me learn to have responsibilities and to be an adult. **MANICHE**

Maniche is a case in point. They met in 2000. The midfielder was 22 at the time and his talent was rebellious. With his future in a limbo: capable of optimising his capacities and developing a top career; but also equally given to being foolish and walking the path into the abyss. The difference between the first possibility – which he eventually adopted – and the second one, may well be explained by the presence of José Mourinho. It may be no coincidence that the highlights of Maniche's career shone precisely in the clubs where he was at the same time as the Special One.

Another episode demonstrating this is told by Maniche himself. It happened during the 2002/03 season, before the first UEFA Cup round that FC Porto would come to win: "We thrashed Poland Warszawa, in the first leg, by 6-0. One week later, Mourinho decided to give most of the team players a rest. The only ones who went to Poland were Postiga and I. I remember it was dead hot and perhaps because of that, among other reasons, we played terribly. At half-time, the result was 0-0, and Mourinho turned to Postiga and said: 'You can book a weekend with your girlfriend because you're not going to be called for the next match.' Then he looked at me and added: 'And you, Maniche, if you think you're going to leave because it's too hot, you're wrong! You're playing the 90 minutes and sweating it out.' At that moment you feel really annoyed with the situation, but the lesson comes later: he wanted my concentration levels up in every game and not just in some. I learned that for good."

TURNING WEAKNESS INTO STRENGTH

José Mourinho knows very well how to take advantage of moments of rupture. He reverses cases of indiscipline in favour of the group, transforming a problem into pedagogy. The targeted players come out stronger and the results show on the pitch. Jorge Costa confirms this: "He liked to set an example for the group through concrete cases. That's how it was with Maniche, Carlos Alberto or

Vítor Baía. But always in a fair way. The punishments were like when a parent reprimands a child." Something similar also happened at the end of 2003, when FC Porto was fighting to access the Champions League eighth-finals. Mourinho didn't like the team's behaviour and caused a small internal hiccup. Costinha was the victim. Before a training session, and in front of the whole group – young players and celebrities -, the coach said to his face that he was no longer counting on him. That he should go talk to the president because he'd stop representing FC Porto at the end of the season. Some say making waves like this was the cornerstone of the season's 'U-turn' and it changed the Dragons' course into a dream, by winning the Champions League.

Faced with Mourinho's tough words, Costinha was piqued. He left the pitch, refusing to participate in the training session. Jorge Costa and Vítor Baía, the two captains, talked to him and managed to bring him round. Costinha came back and was just more mystified: "During training he treated me as if nothing had happened, as if I were just another player, he talked normally without showing any discomfort", the former player recalls. After the session, Costinha and Mourinho met again in the car park, once again with a friendly treatment. Costinha became even more confused: "So in there he lectures me like he did and then he treats me as if nothing had happened?"

The match with Real Madrid at Santiago Bernabéu was approaching. The last one of the Champions League group stage. FC Porto was one step away from the eighth-finals. Costinha would be playing, with a slight catch: if he saw a yellow card, he'd be out of the next match. And it happened, 27 minutes into the game. At the end of the match, Mourinho waited for FC Porto no. 6 player, hugged him and said: "You were brilliant, a truly upright professional!" That moment, Costinha's brain went all dazed.

The eighth-finals. The drawing of the teams. Manchester United. Just days before leaving, Mourinho crosses the training field, notes in hand, and hurriedly goes to a bench where Costinha is resting. In the same breath he starts talking: "We're playing with Manchester United, the first game's here. Fantastic! You can't play because you're being punished, but you can play in the second leg and then you'll be an important piece. Here we'll win 2-0 or 2-1 and there we always score". Costinha's doubts were getting bigger. Was this a wizard before his eyes?

Whether or not he has a crystal ball, I don't know. What I do know is that he communicates with you so deeply and so convincingly that you want to react, even after a sermon like the one I got. **COSTINHA**

On February 25th, 2004, FC Porto beat Manchester United by 2-1, in the Dragon Stadium, as Mourinho had predicted. In the second leg, at Old Trafford, everyone knows what happened, but told by Costinha it has a different flavour: "They scored first and had the qualifying round in their hands until minute 90, when that free kick came up. I asked Maniche to swap positions with me by the entrance to the goal box. I knew O'Shea was tough and, if he had before him a supposedly slower player, like me, he might be more concerned with the ball than with the opponent. That's how it happened. On the rebound the ball ended up with me and I managed to react faster than O'Shea."

FC Porto went on to the quarter-finals with a goal scored by a player whom the coach had marked with a cross three months earlier. A strategic cross, it was later realised. "At the time there was talk about me going to Juventus and Mourinho told me to take it easy. That we were going to win the Champions League and then he'd take me wherever he would go. It was a pact we made which didn't come true for other reasons", reveals Costinha.

THE PRESIDENTS ARE THANKFUL

The code of conduct imposed by José Mourinho only has practical effects with the connivance of the managing structures. This is fundamental and Mourinho makes that very clear from the start. So far, with no exceptions. His disciplining posture has been greatly appreciated by the presidents of the clubs where he's been. "He had his principles of discipline and wouldn't give them up. I think that was a strong point in FC Porto's success because he gained control of the group", says Pinto da Costa. In Real Madrid, Florentino Pérez also had the same feeling: "In Mourinho, I would highlight his professionalism, his leadership and his respect for the values of the centuries-old institution that Real Madrid is."

Pinto da Costa recalls an emblematic episode that shows Mourinho's courage and the perfect harmony between the coach and the administration: "At one point he had a quarrel with Vítor Baía. Mourinho knew Vítor was not only an important player and the team captain, but someone for whom I had a special feeling. I saw the birth of Vítor in FC Porto. I was the one who had his first contract drawn when he was still a player in the Constituição field. So there was a very strong relationship between Vítor and me. But Mourinho didn't let that hinder him. He felt he should punish him and he did. And Vítor didn't play for some time."

On top of this, Baía and Mourinho had a very close relationship, almost like family. When he had that attitude specifically with that player, Mourinho showed the group there were no untouchables "and he left everyone thinking…", concludes Pinto da Costa. Today, ten years on, Vítor Baía looks back at this episode in a curious way: "Knowing better José's way of working, I believe he caused that misunderstanding and led it to escalate, to get more out of my capacities in the future."

Cristiano Ronaldo confirms José Mourinho's disciplining trait. He not only confirms it, but he endorses it:

What I like most about him is the discipline. You can't win anything without discipline. He convinces the players that the first rule to success is discipline. **CRISTIANO RONALDO**

Mourinho's choices are not influenced by status. "The worst thing in a coach is when he shuts his eyes to cases of indiscipline of player 'A', 'B' or 'C' and then he's disciplining when it's player 'D' or 'F'. That gives the impression of a false disciplinarian because he's capable of punishing the less famous ones and sparing the stars. Mourinho uses the same discipline with everyone", guarantees Pinto da Costa. Silvino, the goalkeeper coach, witnessed some cases that prove this equitable profile: "Zé had no problem in saying what he thought to Vítor Baía's face, in FC Porto, or to Eto´o's, in Inter. He looks his players in the eye. When he has something to say, he says it. He doesn't say it behind your back, he says it to your face, whoever you are. Time has proved him right, because both the players at stake and the team always benefitted a lot from this way of being."

"Being surrounded by great players and two top class coaches when he was still an assistant in Barcelona was very important for José Mourinho's preparation as a coach," states Vítor Baía, a contemporary of Mourinho at the Catalan club. The former FC Porto goalkeeper considers this stage of the past to be the root of the disciplinarian that he is today.

> *The disciplinary element, the rigour and the organization – all this he got from van Gaal, who also demanded a lot from the players and even from his assistants, which wasn't very usual at the time.* **VÍTOR BAÍA**

However, once again, José Mourinho knew how to interpret and direct this knowledge towards the group's interests. The Special One is inflexible about applying the rules, but he's not blind when interpreting details that might make a difference. Silvino explains: "Zé really simplifies his relationship with the players. In the changing room, for example, if they want to listen to music or play footvolley, he'll not forbid it. For the sake of discipline, some coaches forbid everything. He doesn't, as long as he understands those things contribute to the players' concentration. And the players love that." Van Gaal couldn't see that far.

DIRECTORS AT ATTENTION!

During each working session, José Mourinho places a tight-knit net around those who are taking part in it, both directly and indirectly. Mourinho's training sessions have to be intense and highly effective. Whoever disturbs those guidelines is asking for trouble…

This is what happened at the start of the 2001/02 season, in Leiria. The technical team led by José Mourinho had only been working for three days. Towards the end of a training session, the thing he wouldn't tolerate actually happened. "The União de Leiria directors were about to play a friendly game with the journalists and they decided to step on the pitch while the training session was still going on. At that moment, Zé stopped everything and started shouting 'Out! Out!' I thought, great, I worked three days and now I'm already leaving – it was good while it lasted", tells assistant Rui Faria.

The truth is the directors left the pitch and returned only when the session had finished. "This episode really shows the professionalism he puts into his job and it made a powerful impression on me, because it showed me straight away what kind of a leader I had", Rui Faria concludes.

A TYPICALLY MILITARY STRATEGY

All businessmen need a plan and a strategy to make things work with the means at their disposal. For many years, I occupied a unique, privileged position to see how people worked and interacted, at the highest level, in a professional football club. I was completely enraptured by José Mourinho, by his attitude and devotion to his work and, in particular, by his impact on the people he interacted and worked with.

Prior to that, I worked for 22 years in an ultra-specialized area, with people linked to strategic planning, both in hostile and peaceful atmospheres. Therefore, I was particularly sensitive to the details concerning this area. It had a great connection to football: the planning in the training session to reach an objective. In order to put a strategy into practice, you must have a certain type of person to carry out plans and action. It's genuine team building, in that you've got to trust our men and motivate them enough to get the best out of them. That's fundamental.

I had the privilege to witness first-hand how Mourinho did that. The way he talked to the players, individually, to find the best way to reach the objective – winning and being the best. The major conclusion I drew from these observations was that, curiously, the way Mourinho works is very similar to the way I used to work to prepare an operation during my time in the army.

Mourinho has the capacity to build in the players a desire, a will and a belief, which get them to realise their best performance ever. His greatest skill, in my opinion, is being able to communicate with any person of any level, from the greenest beginner to the most senior member. The way he manages to bring everyone towards a common objective, together with his capacity to plan and to prepare for any eventuality, makes him a very special person.

It's a mistake to say José Mourinho is an arrogant man. True, he doesn't hide the confidence he has in his own capacities; but he's also one of the humblest and most sensitive men I've ever met. He's not afraid to make decisions, his procedures are bold, and if something is not working he's quick to react and correct the situation. It's as if he's always got a Plan B, or even a Plan C.

I found many similarities between carrying out a successful military operation and the way José works in football. He instils discipline and has a strong sense of self-discipline. He encourages respect and trust between all members of the group. He contributes to an understanding between his assistants and makes them believe they can perform their tasks with will, passion and faith.

In the armed forces, your life and the lives of the others often depend on each one's capacity to reach the objective, which is to win. When I worked with José, I realised that not only the players, but all the team members, including those backstage, had that mentality. And he could get the best out of each and every one of them. I'm proud to have been able to witness José's work.

He didn't shout. He'd choose a more eloquent way to express himself: charisma. José is charismatic. And that's how he got the players and the staff to believe in his plan.

Another essential feature of José Mourinho is his will to win. That's crucial in football or in a military operation. José has that will in his blood and manages to convey it in a subconscious manner to those surrounding him.

BRIAN HORRIGAN

I KNEW you WORE SPECIAL
BEFORE you TOLD THE WORLD
PRESS !!. NOW you HAVE LEFT
ENGLAND EVERyone WANTS THE
SPECIAL one BACK
Your FRIEND PETER

Dedication by Peter Kenyon

MOTIVATION...

Hi Boss, I could spend all day long talking about you and it still wouldn't be enough. I have the best memories of working with you, we still keep in touch and I'm very pleased about that. Thanks for everything you did for me, you know I deeply respect you. I hope to see you again, and who knows, to work with you again. Good luck!

FRANK LAMPARD

Mourinho has the merit of getting such good people to go running after a ball.

JUAN IGNACIO MARTÍNEZ

Mourinho was already born with 'mo'tivation in his name. He's the first to admit it, several times throughout his career: "My motivation is top level." Meaning: "... it's winning". But Mourinho doesn't just want to win. In fact, he does win. One triumph after another keeps up his motivation, but mainly that of those surrounding him.

José Mourinho's presence is a source of motivation for his players, but also for... his opponents. A few days after having signed with Real Madrid, the first reaction of Xavi, captain of the main rival, confirmed this contention: "Being from Barcelona, and given my force in the group, to me Mourinho's arrival is like an extra motivation." Everyone wants to beat Mourinho, first and foremost, and only then the club that Mourinho coaches. Few coaches have gained such importance in world football.

Mourinho's enthusiasm contaminates the players even before they are working with him. For instance, the power of words was very clear to Didier Drogba. The Ivory Coast player had just finished a marvellous season in Marseilles, reaching the goalkeepers' vice-leadership and winning the status of best player in the French championship. José Mourinho had just signed with Chelsea and was looking for someone just like Drogba. But he didn't just ask and then sit there waiting for the transfer to be concluded. He hopped on a plane and went to meet the player with an irresistible speech: "When Chelsea thought about hiring me, he came to me and told me: 'If you want to be a great attacker like Thierry Henri or Ruud van Niestelroy you've got to come to England and play with me in Chelsea'. He convinced me to sign with Chelsea", reveals Drogba. The attacker was grateful for the rest of his life: "He went looking for me! OK, so I was a good player in the French championship, but he made me one of the best players in Europe. Today I feel proud, because thanks to him I reached the level of the finest players. That's why I'd go to the end of the world for José."

For Marco Materazzi, motivation came via… a text message. 22nd June, 2008. European Championship quarter-finals. The Italian team had just been eliminated by Spain in a dramatic game, decided by penalty kicks (4-2). Devastated, Materazzi left the Ernst Happel field. When he got to the booths, a surprise.

I was still taking my boots off in the changing room when the phone rang. It was a message from José Mourinho. It said for me not to feel discouraged, to move on, because I had to prepare myself to start winning in Inter. It's an example of how he tries to be close to us from the start on the good days, but particularly on the bad days. **MATERAZZI**

Mourinho, just contracted by Inter, was on holiday. He could have waited for Materazzi to return to the club, but his message of comfort wouldn't have had the same effect. This way, he won over the heart of a player who, two years on, wept like a child on the Portuguese coach's shoulder when he left Inter.

Dejan Stankovic was also impressed at first contact. The Serb had been in Inter since 2004, but the last few seasons hadn't been exactly sunny. Some irritating injuries had been compromising the midfielder's talent. José Mourinho made a point of personally telling Stankovic that he was counting on him for the new cycle: "I remember that first meeting we had. After five minutes of conversation I was ready to take on the world." At this stage of his career, the Serb was already past his prime. So he was even more impressed with the teachings he received: "I learned a lot with him. I learned things that, being 30, I thought I already knew. I grew up a lot with him, not just as a player, but also as a man. He was the best coach I ever had."

With words like these, the question is: why is the motivation conveyed by Mourinho so effective and so deep? Stankovic himself gives us important clues on this: "It's a unique way of doing things, of facing easy or difficult situations. It's the knack he has to understand us, to get inside our heads and win us over." And, not least, "he's not one of those who uses you and then discards you", the Serb concludes.

Mourinho is remarkably persuasive when talking. The players absorb and process the message. In the face of different realities, the Portuguese coach knows how to choose the right approach and gist for each situation. This is what Cristiano Ronaldo tells us in a simpler way: "I love working with Zé because I really like the way he talks to the players."

José Morais, Mourinho's assistant, gives a better explanation of this caring relationship: "He holds the players accountable for what their job is and at the same time he frees them because he helps them find solutions. He's always sensitive to each one's problems." Mourinho's motivational strategy is developed by stages, with no end in sight.

"When he realises a certain player has reached the proposed level, he immediately sets the bar higher, meaning, what we've done is extraordinary but now we've got to go higher and give it even more." It's a constant, daily boost, that can happen, for instance, at half-time during a game: "I've seen situations where he calls a certain player, praises the work he's done so far but adds: 'You're a great player, you've run and worked hard, but you haven't shot on the goal!' And the athlete goes back on the pitch thinking about that", concludes José Morais.

IN THE OFFICE OR IN THE SHOWER

When José Mourinho landed in London to coach Chelsea, the club had already hired a young prodigy for goalkeeper: Petr Cech. The Czech, who'd come from modest Rennes, had cost 7 million pounds and was looked upon as a medium-term replacement for the Italian Carlo Cudicini, who had just entered his thirties.

Cech confesses that "all I wanted was a place in the team, because I was 22 years old and the undisputed goalkeeper was Carlo Cudicini". But Mourinho's arrival turned Cech's head and changed his plans. "I got to Chelsea's training centre, which was in Arlington at the time, he called me to his office and told me we were at the start of a stage and everyone took off on equal conditions. 'Are you ready to fight for a place?', he asked me. I firmly answered I was, because I felt he would give the same opportunities to everyone", reveals Petr Cech.

The young goalkeeper was ecstatic. He realised the distance between himself and the place as team goalkeeper was in his hands. "I knew it would only depend on me and on what I did in the pre-season. It was a decisive boost for my career", says Cech. The result is public knowledge. Weeks later Mourinho called Cech to inform him he was to field at the start of the season. Thus Chelsea gained a goalkeeper for life, with a simple conversation in the office. That season of 2004/05, he went for 25 games without conceding goals (1,025 minutes) and was considered the best player in the world between the posts.

A similar motivational recipe was used with Frank Lampard, also in Chelsea. Before Mourinho's arrival, the English international's talent was already indisputable. But the idea also prevailed that his performance on the pitch was below his potential. "I my mind, all I wanted was to be a good English player, I didn't think I could be a world top player", he confesses. Lampard needed a plus to set him off, and in came Mourinho: "One day, in the changing room, I was taking a shower and he approached me with Silvino and said:

"You're the best player in the World." I was speechless. He added: "But you need to win trophies, like Zidane, to be acknowledged like he is." I left the changing rooms feeling 10 foot high. **FRANK LAMPARD**

Or, as we say in football jargon, full of 'morale': "Obviously I wasn't the best in the World, but with those words he made he feel like a special player. At that moment I thought: this coach is going to take me wherever he wants to."

Lampard had already been wearing the Blues' colours for three years, always coached by the Italian Claudio Ranieri. But, when we're talking about José Mourinho, the best advice is "forget everything you've learned so far". There was a total transformation: "I could give you many examples about the good things Mourinho brought me – tactical aspects, technical issues, and so on. But the most important thing he did for me was to give me a new character and make me believe in myself. The moment we started working, my career took a new turn", the Chelsea midfielder concluded.

Cech and Lampard are just two examples of a surgical motivational work which, in a mere three years and a few months, changed Chelsea into a top England and world football club. In a short time he built a football machine, without prejudices, ready to take on the world. All of it founded on heavily motivational bases, as captain John Terry recalls: "When he got here we started holding hands or hugging each other in a circle, before the games. He'd say a few words and at the end we'd shout: Chelsea! Chelsea! Chelsea! This brought us closer together instantly."

With Mourinho, Chelsea regained the champion's title after 50 years, then revalidated it, and still won another four cups and reached two Champions League semi-finals.

THE INFERIORITY COMPLEX

One of Mourinho's crucial tasks was to eliminate the inferiority complex the Blues had entrenched in their history. That's why all the players highlight the almost unconscious confidence revealed by the Portuguese coach before the major games. "For instance, in the Champions League quarter-finals or semi-finals, situations in which the players were very tense and nervous, José would walk into the changing room, really relaxed, and wholeheartedly say: 'Today we're going to win 2-0.' And suddenly all that tension vanished", says Frank Lampard. Their confidence increased while Mourinho's guesses kept matching the results. And that happened a lot.

Internally, the task was also huge. Manchester United and Arsenal had won 11 championships in the previous 12 years. The Red Devils, with eight titles and a football legend – Sir Alex Ferguson – at the helm, seemed a target impossible to hit. Chelsea was destined for a secondary role, living in a permanent inferiority complex. José

Mourinho treated this disease with confidence injections, as simple as they were effective: "At first we were surprised because in the big games, against Manchester United or Arsenal, we were naturally concerned, but he had the gift of making easy something difficult."

Petr Cech, John Terry, Frank Lampard and Didier Drogba were chosen by Mourinho to form the backbone of Chelsea. Everything revolved around these four men, on and off the pitch. The group followed them. Mourinho used them as an example, but he also exposed them when the circumstances required it. Drogba remembers no-one was spared: "On several occasions he came to me, after the games, to say: 'Didier, today you didn't play well...' And I'd work even harder to please him. Motivation-wise, he's simply the best. I always gave my all to my coaches. To all of them. But he was special."

Individual conversations are actually not that common in the motivation process adopted by Mourinho. As Rui Faria explains, the Portuguese coach only resorts to that in very specific cases: "It only happens in extremely important, decisive games, not regularly. It's when he sees fit. And sometimes he even delegates that mission to his assistants. He prefers us to transmit things which strategically he doesn't want to be the one to say."

Mourinho doesn't throw away gestures or words. Each intervention has an objective. "The objective is almost always to motivate the player", says Costinha, "but that can happen through various concepts: exposure, humiliation, praise – it depends on the circumstances."

Petr Ceca keeps a personal memory regarding this topic. The 2006/07 season was just taking off. The Czech goalkeeper was recovering from a surgery on his shoulder. He resumed training on a Friday, after a long stop, and Chelsea was playing against Blackburn the following day, for the third round of the Premier League. With half a dozen words and a gesture, Mourinho gave him back a mountain of confidence: "I'd just finished training with

Silvino and we'd only done shooting on the goal. It went terribly. At every shot a goal was scored! José came up to me and asked: 'Are you ready to play tomorrow?' I replied: 'Boss, I haven't been training, today was my first day in a goal and honestly I don't think I'm prepared to play.' He paused, looked at me and said: 'Don't worry, if you don't want to play there's no problem, we'll talk again tomorrow, you're on, you're travelling with us and then we'll see. I want you to be part of the team, to feel the atmosphere.'"

The team travelled to Blackburn with two goalkeepers, Petr Cech and Carlo Cudicini. On the morning of the match, at breakfast, Mourinho approached the Czech again and got the same answer: "Nothing's changed, Boss, I don't feel up to it". The surprise came in the afternoon. "During the lecture, I see my name among the starting lineup. I was amazed! But at the same time I thought he wouldn't call me up if he wasn't sure I could do it. If he had confidence in me, I'd also have to have it", says Cech. Chelsea had a great performance, winning 2-0, and the Blues' number 1 didn't concede any goals. "It's an episode I'm going to remember forever."

THE GROUP AND THE VIDEOS

It's during group talks that José Mourinho strengthens ties and consolidates the 'family'. "What's most touching about him is the way he got on with the group", confirms Costinha. "In the trips we made back to Oporto, at the back of the bus there was a space where only the older players would get together. Often he'd turn up and sit down for a while to talk. It's funny because we had our own snacks and he made a point of paying for his own snack to join in our conversations. The next thing we knew, he was another one of us. He'd stay there a while and then go, discreetly, the same way he'd arrived."

If need be, Mourinho reinvents motivation. This happened when preparing for the famous Champions League semi-final in the 2009/10 season, when Inter eliminated Barcelona. The situation was sinister for the Italian team. No-one bet a dime on Inter's victory against the Culer "football demolition machine". During the lecture devoted to the videos on the opponent's virtues, the coach surprised everyone: he reversed it all.

In the first video, instead of showing the usual - the opponent's qualities - he showed images of their group stage, with examples of Barcelona's frailties. This detail immediately transmitted to the players the idea that if they made mistakes, maybe we could seize the opportunity and win. **RUI FARIA**

The trick had the power of turning around what the players thought about the game. The result was what we know.

In FC Porto videos had a double function: to show prime moves made by the opponent and to relax the audience. "His powerpoints were very short, 10 to 15 minutes, so as not to bore anyone. He liked to finish with some funny photo collages of the players, just to relax. But it's curious that he never let one of himself be made. I tried several times to do his with my collaborators, but they never let me: 'No way, the Boss doesn't like it, you can't do one with him', they'd say", tells Costinha.

The 'relaxation' factor is almost always present, especially in the more tense moments. Costinha recalls another episode during the lecture before the game between FC Porto and Real Madrid for the Champions League. Mourinho said goodbye to his players with the following phrase: "Now don't forget to go out and ask those guys for autographs. The only thing they have better than you is money in their bank account, that they've got plenty more than any one of us here. As for the football, that's up to you."

A LESSON "À LA GREEK"

The most striking example of motivation imposed by José Mourinho took place on 13th March, 2003. FC Porto had just lost by 0-1, in the Antas Stadium, against Panathinaikos. It was the first leg of the UEFA Cup quarter-finals. The Pole Emmanuel Olisadebe shook FC Porto's European dream, when there were only 17 minutes to full-time.

The Dragons fought to the death, they created loads of opportunities to undo their disadvantage, but they didn't manage. As soon as the Italian Domenico Messina blew the final whistle, José Mourinho jumped like a spring towards the opponents' bench, where the players were celebrating enthusiastically. He greeted the coach, Sergio Markarian and, pointing his finger at them, he warned: "Don't celebrate too much because this isn't over yet!"

Then he hurriedly walked across the field, passed Chainho – a substitute for Panathinaikos who hadn't been used in that game, and who'd been a player for FC Porto before – and repeated the idea: "You can tell those mates of yours, who are all happy, that we're going to win in Greece!" And he finished his round passing by the

Super Dragon supporters, raising and lowering his arms, the palms of his hands wide open, recommending peace and ensuring confidence. Vítor Baía, who was at the time the leading goalkeeper for FC Porto, has no doubt: "He began to prepare the game in Greece while he was still on the Antas stadium pitch."

In a wise, anticipatory way, José Mourinho foresaw the terrible inhospitable environment of Athens – where Panathinaikos hadn't lost in European competitions for eight years – and he began the psychological work that would be instrumental to face the second match. It was a spontaneous reaction in time, but calculated in actions.

Work with the FC Porto players ensued, while still at the stadium. Pinto da Costa witnessed this: "I have his image in the changing room, insistently telling the players to be calm and that we were going there to win", says the president.

After the game against Panathinaikos, which we lost by 1-0 at home, he got to the changing room and yelled: "Whoever doesn't believe we're going to Greece to win and go on had better not go!" The truth is we won 0-2 on a really tough pitch where they hadn't lost in eight years. **DECO**

A profound disappointment lingered in the blue and white changing room. It seemed impossible to reconstruct the ruins of the team in due time. But Mourinho's words were a genuine balm. "The group felt that they represented the enormous confidence he had in us and, above all, in himself" – says Deco – "He could convey that in an incredible, perhaps unique, way."

Vítor Baía recalls the magical reaction of the group those following days: "Suddenly, and unexpectedly, we gained this huge confidence and assurance. So much so, that after the game, we went for dinner with our families and friends and we were already commenting with one another how we were going to win in Greece for sure. Those closest to us reacted with total surprise: 'How can you have all that confidence when you've just lost a game?' It had everything to do with him, with our leader and with the message he got through to us."

The truth is, a week later, the team entered one of the toughest stadiums in Europe, facing a totally hostile atmosphere, and performed a perfect game. Derlei tied the qualifying round very early on – in the 15th minute – and scored again in extra time, thus passing to the semi-final. FC Porto was on its way to conquering the UEFA Cup, José Mourinho's first European trophy.

THE MILL CAN'T STOP GRINDING

When I think about Mourinho, what first comes to my mind is his fabulous personality. I've always felt that great leaders are bound to have a great personality. And José has that very assertive, strong characteristic. It's a sort of personality turned towards the world. This is how you can understand better why the teams he runs have so much personality. It's a virtue that starts with him.

All the teams commanded by José are motivated. All of them try to win, always. All of them have a method, a tactic. And all of them try to comply with his scheme 100%. That means he can motivate the teams easily.

From my own experience, I say the issue of motivation is not an easy one, whether we're talking about the coach's motivation to keep winning, or the players' to stay competitive. I've won many trophies and I've worked with a lot of equally winning players. Therefore, experience tells me that there is no recipe for motivation that you can apply equally to a group. Every case is unique. It's up to the leader to have the sensibility required to understand what the appropriate dose is, at a specific moment and for a specific player.

When exaggerated, motivation becomes over-motivation and can become a hindrance. In such a case, the players become tense because the message is excessive for their expectations.

Hence the need to have in-depth knowledge of the athletes, so as to give them the right motivation. Sometimes it takes no more than a couple of words. Realising this is vital. José has that talent. He knows when and how to motivate his players.

I look at José and I identify with many of his attitudes. Right in the first year, in Chelsea, when I saw him launching into those sprints by the touch line, at Old Trafford, I was reminded of my early days in Aberdeen, jumping, punching the air, celebrating. It's only human! You can't hide your emotions. They're always there, they're part of you, of your character. And you can't change your character just because the context is a football match. On the contrary. Usually, people's character emerges in spontaneous situations: when a goal is scored, or a goal is missed, for example. Everything José did – even if we didn't appreciate it – were his emotions, not a form of provocation. It reminds me of my early days as a coach.

It's not during the game that you meet people in depth. There important personality traits come to the surface, but you can't judge someone just on that. When I had the chance to know José Mourinho better, it was during the moments after the games. In the company of a bottle of wine, we shared some amusing situations. He laughs about himself, he doesn't take himself too seriously, and he's got a great sense of humour. I'd tease him, provoke him, and he'd play along. On several occasions, after the games, we sat and relaxed talking about different things, other than the competition.

I always enjoyed those moments with him. Our life as coaches doesn't allow for regular meetings. Sometimes we'd go four or five months without seeing each other, but whenever he turned up for a drink after a game, it was a great moment. No matter what the result had been. He always accepted the fact that you can win or lose. He always understood that.

The first time we met for a drink was at the end of a home match in Chelsea. The wine they served was awful! I turned to José and asked him: "What the hell is this? Paint remover? You use this to take paint off the doors, don't you?" He burst out laughing... At that moment Abramovich walked in and José told him: "This wine's dreadful! We shouldn't serve this to human beings..." Everyone laughed about this episode. José concluded it with the phrase: "From now on, only Barca Velha!" He's a great friend.

Yet, despite this friendship, the only thing I can't guarantee to José is a place as coach for Manchester United. For the simple reason that I don't intend to retire. Or rather, I don't want to retire. The problem about getting old and considering retirement is thinking: "What am I going to do then?" Any person's occupation is like a mill: while you're working, the mill's in a good state; you stop and the mill goes into ruins. Stopping the mill is dangerous to your health. Therefore, José, my intention is to keep working. I hope you do the same.

And one more thing: you know exactly the quality of the wine I like... See if you bring an even better one next time!

ALEX FERGUSON

Jose,
I trust that my words for your book are OK with you, I have told the truth about our strong relationships and also for our love of the best wine!
So until the next glass, good luck
Alex.

Dedication by Alex Ferguson

BROTHERHOOD...

Boss, from the bottom of my heart I tell you it was a pleasure to work with you. We're still in touch and I hope that, some-day, we'll work again together side by side – you never know.

JOHN TERRY

Mourinho is spectacular. Not many know this, but he can be your father, your older brother, your teacher... and that's really important to a player.

JERZY DUDEK

The title of this chapter was chosen with special care. More than a friend of the players, José Mourinho is a 'brother'. He's one of them. The athletes recognise his hierarchical legitimacy, but they know he's their peer whenever the circumstances so justify. Mourinho is the first one to assume the mea culpa when the group's honour is threatened.

At any rate, brotherhood is a word that is expressed as a concept in the very first article of the Declaration of Human Rights: "All human beings are born free and equal in dignity and rights. They are endowed with reason and conscience and should act towards one another in a spirit of brotherhood."

I'm sure Mourinho doesn't practice brotherhood for having read the universal declaration. He does so because it's the only intelligent way of dealing with 23 or 24 other human beings, on a daily basis, during many consecutive months. The players need to feel the presence of someone who is capable of pushing the world for them. In their name. Mourinho is that kind of person. As Costinha recalls:

Mourinho would say: "If any player of mine is in the pits no-one's going to step on him, we're all going to give him a hand and pull him up." In those moments we need everyone. **COSTINHA**

The motto is valid in all circumstances, for all protagonists and at all moments. Defending the group is defending your own honour.

Peter Kenyon, former chief executive of Chelsea, personally experienced glaring examples of this brotherhood: "It was amazing how he managed to create an atmosphere of protection for the players. José would absorb all the criticism made by the journalists, by managers or even by other coaches regarding his own players. He was a protective shield for the team, even overriding his own ambition. And there were times, many times, that he paid a heavy price for this, because he became everyone's focus of attention."

Marco Materazzi actually uses the terms "father" or "older brother" to describe the type of relationship Mourinho establishes with the players. "He shows he's willing to 'die' for us, just like a father or an older brother does. And when I say 'us', I mean not only the players who play regularly, but also those who aren't on the eleven, as was my case: a substitute and, on top of that, team captain. When I start a coaching career I'm going to look back on the example José gave me, especially regarding the psychological dimension."

It's likely that José Mourinho got this brotherly concern from one of his masters, Bobby Robson. Vítor Baía worked with both, in Barcelona, and he's sure of this: "He absorbed this ability to deal with the players from Bobby Robson, who was known exactly for that. The image Mr. Robson passed onto the players was exactly that. And at that time Mourinho already got on really well with us."

AFFECTION

Jorge Mendes is a privileged confidant of the players. Besides managing careers, he also manages emotions and follows lives. The entrepreneur has heard, countless times, expressions of gratitude and affection directed at José Mourinho. "No player – and you know my relationship with many of them – not one, ever made any criticism about him. All of them, without exception, consider him a genius", says Mendes. Mourinho's presence in a project is a pole of attraction and a premium business card for any club. "The amount of players in other clubs who's confessed to me how they'd like to work with him… And those who have already worked with him, when he leaves, want to go with him as well because they're sure they can win again. Everyone reckons that Zé is different", says Mendes.

Affection can be a justification for the magnet effect he has on the players. Diego Milito confirms this.

When I talk about him I talk about affection. I was impressed from the very first moment, when I spoke to him over the phone before coming to Inter. He called me, we spoke a little and I immediately realised he was a special coach. Mourinho gave me a lot, personally and professionally. He had unique details with me. **DIEGO MILITO**

The mark of affection remains forever. A recent interview by Wesley Sneijder to the Italian newspaper La Gazzetta dello Sport proves this. The Dutch Inter player admits there's no other coach like Mourinho. "I know it's useless, but we keep looking for a coach with something of Mourinho's, there's no-one else like him, no-one knows how to treat the players like he does", said Sneijder. A declaration of affection stronger than this one would be hard to make.

That's why the Dutch international views the parade of coaches in Inter after Mourinho's departure as natural (Benítez, Leonardo, Gasperini and now Ranieri): "Arriving after Mourinho would be difficult for anyone, not just for Benítez." José Mourinho is different, he's unique.

The affection transmitted by José Mourinho is genuine and true. There is abundant proof of this, with a wide range of witnesses. The opposite image of the one the Portuguese coach transmits to the public. People who don't know him label him as being arrogant, but that's only until you have a first contact with him. Confirmation of this is offered by the reputable Diego Maradona: "I went to the Inter training centre as Argentine national coach. I hadn't met José Mourinho. I was talking to the goalkeeper Júlio César when he came over and told me to make myself comfortable because I was in my home. Then we spoke about football and I rapidly realised he already knew everything about my work, everything I wanted for Argentina, all the players I was going to call up… he knew more than me." The big surprise for Maradona happened later, when they said goodbye: "He gave me a rosary and said: 'This job's tough but I wish you the best for your career.' I found him to be an exceptional man." Another unequivocal gesture of brotherhood.

Pinto da Costa had also experienced a similar episode: "The first year we were champions, we also won the Portugal Cup. At the end of the match, Mourinho turned to me, offered me a rosary and said: 'President, this is for you because it accompanied me in all the games.' At that moment he proved to be a person of great sensibility and feeling, which bears no relation to the arrogant portrait that many make of him", says the president of FC Porto.

Abraham Lincoln once said that "you can fool some of the people all the time, all the people some of the time, but you cannot fool all the people all the time." That's why so many players have been saying the same thing for so long. Mourinho fools no-one.

The feeling is mutual. When he hears compliments such as Milito's, Mourinho looks at himself in the mirror:

If you ask me to talk about any of my former players, I'm sure my emotions will be no different from those with which they talk about me. **JOSÉ MOURINHO**

Mourinho goes on: "Wherever we've been we've had fantastic people working with us. Generally speaking, we manage to build empathy with the people we work with. Not just the players, but also those in charge of the medical departments, kit staff… all the people that belong to the club, including the fans. It's our way of being, it's the honesty with which we do things, the dedication and the ambition. People feel there's a strong commitment in the determination with which we devote ourselves to our activities. And they come with us."

It is worth referring once again to the theme of this chapter: brotherhood. It is after the affection transmitted by Mourinho that the players run. He leaves strong friendships wherever he goes. Genuine 'fraternities' are created. Mourinho's not just a coach, he's a real human Swiss army knife: manager, psychologist, confidant and friend. A "type of person" with whom Frank Lampard had never had contact before 2004:

He was the first coach with whom I felt at ease to talk about my private life, my girlfriend and my kids. **FRANK LAMPARD**

"It was that relationship that made my work with him easier. I felt he truly respected me as a human being. He was very approachable", concludes Lampard.

But, as with all trusted friends, Mourinho doesn't just say what's pleasant to hear. He gives with one hand and hands over responsibility with the other. Lampard was even asked this question:

"Do you want to play on Sunday or would you rather rest?" It was enough for the England international to feel "important and stimulated". In Stankovic's case, the 'offer' was even greater:

> *When we won the first championship, three rounds from the end, he came to me and said: "Take your wife and go to Dubai for a week, you don't need to come in to train. You've worked so hard for me and for the team that you deserve seven days' rest. His gesture touched me.* **STANKOVIC**

These are touching gestures, but they also make the players accountable: "He can give some days' rest to a player, but when that player comes back he'll tell him: 'Now you're going to give me your game, and show me your worth.' And the player does it even more willingly, he gives his all, he makes more and more of an effort because he knows that next time he'll be rewarded", says Drogba.

BEING THERE IN THE DIFFICULT HOURS

His friendship has often been put to the test during these 11 years. José Mourinho never let anyone down. Even in his early coaching days, when inexperience might affect even the noblest of feelings.

The first test of unconditional solidarity happened in October 2003. César Peixoto had been expressly requested by Mourinho during the preparation of the 2002/03 season. The first year was troubled. The coach thought the left-handed player's dedication was insufficient and he never considered him a full member of the first team. In 2003/04 everything changed. Peixoto responded to the demands and was placed in the first line of choices. When everything seemed to be on track, the player suffers a knee ligament rupture during a match with Boavista. A serious injury. To date, the most serious injury of a player coached by Mourinho. It was the latter, visibly shaken, who broke the news to the media:

"It's a serious injury. It's not recoverable for Monday or for a long time. It's the first time such a serious injury has happened to a player of mine, since I've been a coach, and it's a very strange feeling. Because I can't count on a player for a long time and because it's César, I feel a great sadness."

The season had only begun three months before. It was certain that the team would be deprived of one player almost until the end of the season. The winter market looked like the logical solution. But Mourinho was quick to assure that he wasn't going to look for a replacement for César Peixoto. The proof of respect towards the player and the group went further. A few days later, José Mourinho made a point of being present at the athlete's surgical intervention, thus following in loco every step of the sad affair.

There was no history of such an attitude in Portuguese football, not even in international football. Mourinho's character was a surprise, once again. Everyone realised, in and out, that no player of his was a disposable object. Ever.

Two months later, another predicament for the Porto team. Derlei, one of the crucial elements in winning the Championship and the UEFA Cup the previous season, suffered an anterior cruciate ligament knee injury. One more player for whom the season went up in smoke. José Mourinho went back to being a friend in the difficult hours. He was in the operating room of the Ordem da Trindade Hospital, he watched the surgery and on the microphones he turned weakness into strength: "All us of want to get to the end of the season and say that, even without Derlei, we were champions. We don't want to say we weren't because we lost him. We want to be champions and I'm convinced we're going to be."

Petr Cech has a similar story to tell, in England. Who doesn't remember the terrible injury the Czech goalkeeper suffered in October 2006? Cech dived at Stephen Hunt's feet and ended up knocking his head violently against the Reading player's knee. The collision caused a depression in his skull and the post-operative period put him on sick leave for three months. The most visible recollection of this episode is a protective helmet that Petr Cech has to wear to this day, on medical advice, during training and in the matches. Faced with this misfortune, José Mourinho was a surprise, again.

When I injured myself seriously, he came to see me at the hospital and brought everyone along. All the players came to talk to me after the surgery. At that moment you realise how everyone worries about you. **PETR CECH**

But Mourinho's noble gestures carried on: "I remember that, publicly, he tried to improve the rules concerning medical healthcare procedures for the players in the stadiums. It was clear he effectively wanted to improve things", says Petr Cech. "During my recovery period, when I was training, he'd often ask me if things were going well and if I felt comfortable. It was really good to feel that, to feel that people were taking care of me, especially him."

José Mourinho never played football on a high competitive level, nor did he personally ever suffer a bad injury. But he didn't need to go through that himself to know that, in an athlete's life, there's nothing more distressing than a stop caused by injury. Like the one that happened to Costinha, in 2002/03, on the eve of leaving for Rome, where FC Porto was playing against Lazio for access to the UEFA Cup final. During one of the training sessions in preparation for the decisive game, after winning 4-1 at home, Marco Ferreira accidentally hit Costinha in the nose, causing a head injury: "It was such a trauma for me. I'd never played in Italy, it was my dream. Furthermore, it was a decisive game. My wife says she's never seen me cry so much. On the way to the hospital, semi-conscious, she says I kept asking the doctors to let me play." José Mourinho realised how deep the disappointment was and, taking advantage of the fact that he was being punished, he

immediately found a way to ease the athlete's pain by placing him 'inside' the game. Mourinho on the bench and Costinha in a hospital bed: "We spent the whole game exchanging messages about tactical details, about which were the best choices to make, about how we could reach a result that would get us to the final."

Paulo Ferreira recalls another episode where Mourinho once again revealed all his compassion: "I remember perfectly the time when I lost my father, I was playing for FC Porto, and it was Mourinho himself who said: 'Paulo, you go and come back only when you're up to it. Stay as long as you need with your family.' Most people don't know this side of Mourinho. He's always with the players, he helps us in any way we need and we know we have to give back everything he does for us."

DRAMATIC GOODBYES

In the euphoria of victory, the fans are still celebrating inside Santiago Bernabéu. Inter has just beaten Bayern Munich 2-0, regaining the Champions after 45 years. Outside the stadium, after scores of interviews, José Mourinho sits in the back of a dark luxury car, where his family is already. The door closes, the car pulls off. At a crossroads close by, near the Inter bus, is a tall man, equipped with a tracksuit and leaning against the wall. He seems crushed. It's Materazzi. Mourinho notices him and asks to get out of the car, after a mere ten metres' drive. He moves towards the man, with a firm step. They meet. Mourinho puts his right arm around his neck, Materazzi does the same, pulling the coach's head against his chest. Both cry convulsively. These are 30 seconds of extreme human intensity. Mourinho turns around and shows his face disfigured by emotion. Materazzi, still leaning against the wall, lifts up his head, trying to stop the tears. The coach goes down the street, gets into the dark car and goes his own way.

These images were seen around the world. The toughest of players and the coldest of coaches showed, without a script, that all that was one big lie. That, contrary to what people thought, neither one nor the other had a heart of stone. Materazzi explains this:

I'm a tough, strong man, but that day my heart was on fire. That hug epitomised two great years. He was part of a family, he was the leader of a family that was always ready to face everything and everyone. **MATERAZZI**

Materazzi concludes that "it was what we did. And we managed to bring home the Champions Cup. That moment I was sad, he touched my heart because he was special to me." Minutes earlier, Mourinho had done all he could for Materazzi to play in the final, even if for only a few moments, and he'd succeeded. The defender entered three minutes before the end and thanked him for the rest of his life: "I'd already played in a World Cup final and I'd been champion. Adding to that historical moment my participation in a Champions final was really important to me. He realised this and gave me the opportunity. On the other hand, he knew about my history in Inter, he knew how important I was in the club and he wanted to give me the chance to participate in the dream of all Interistas. This shows his sense of justice and how he appreciated and respected me. It was a grand gesture."

This scene starring Materazzi was emblematic because it was filmed, seen all over the world and had a huge public impact. But, to say the truth, it was no different from so many other scenes lived with other players, other clubs, but kept within the privacy of the group.

Javier Zanetti, for example, also cried that day, while he was still on the field: "For 15 years I'd been waiting for that moment, for the privilege of raising the Champions Cup as team captain. It was really important to me."

Amidst the celebrations we exchanged heartfelt words, with mutual sincerity. Then we hugged and cried because we'd become very good friends. I already knew he was going to Madrid. **ZANETTI**

The farewell moment is always the most painful part of José Mourinho's professional relationships. No-one can accept that someone, with whom they've built such a strong brotherly relationship over the years and months, is going away.

The farewell to Chelsea was another one of those moments. Didier Drogba remembers "there was a lot of emotion in the changing room the day he came to say goodbye to us. It seemed unreal, as if it weren't true, like a film, because we saw him every day and we weren't prepared to see him go. It was a shock. I really felt the Mister's departure and I confess it wasn't easy to find my way back into the competition."

One thing Drogba doesn't confess, but Paulo Ferreira says the Ivory Coast player was in tears that day.

It would be going too far to claim that the farewell to Chelsea was the most emotional. José Mourinho also left behind strong bonds in Benfica, in União de Leiria, in FC Porto, in Inter and in Real Madrid. However, as Paulo Ferreira explains, in Chelsea it was different: "Unlike most of the other clubs where he worked, Chelsea was never a very big club. It had money but it didn't win much. Zé's arrival changed everything. We built a team, a family. Every year we won something. We really enjoyed putting Chelsea up where it is today."

Saying goodbye is always complicated, but that one was even harder. He came to the changing room, gathered us all and said he was leaving. He said he'd miss the good times we'd had and he hugged us, one by one. I remember Didier (Drogba) cried like a child. **PAULO FERREIRA**

José Mourinho's empathy with the Chelsea stars was instantaneous. Lampard says "it wasn't long before the club benefitted from the creation of a strong group spirit. You could tell how the players loved and respected him, both those who played and those who were substitutes. He built a really strong belief in us. All of us, without exception, were proud to be part of a successful team."

It was painful to undo the 'family'. In Paulo Ferreira's specific case, it was even harder: "I was with him for six years, not six days. We created a very strong connection. In my case, in Didier's (Drogba), in Ricardo Carvalho's, among others, we came to Chelsea because he insisted."

MAXIMUM AUTHORITY

The 'Mourinho family' is built on a good mood and respect. Mourinho is the main instigator of laughter. He lays himself bare, provides confidence and goes much further than what would be conventional in a leader. A risk that most coaches never take, fearing to lose their authority. "He doesn't think that way. He has no problem in creating a relationship with the players. He talks about everything, fools around, tells jokes, without any fear of losing control of the situation. He creates such a positive family atmosphere that when he demands maximum concentration the players commit themselves one hundred per cent." The difference between medicine and poison has always been the size of the dose, and José Mourinho knows how to administer the right doses.

Neither a tight rein, nor a whip. With Mourinho everything is simple. "Too normal", as Silvino says. "If the players want to listen to music in the changing room, he'll not forbid it, if they want to play foot-volley in the changing room, he'll not forbid it. As long as the players feel all right, he authorises it", the goalkeeper coach concludes. Silvino gives practical examples: "In Chelsea the players loved to listen to music. In Inter they didn't. Here in Real Madrid they also love to listen to music before we go on the field. We go to warm-up and when we come back Zé likes to talk for a couple of minutes. That's when we turn off the music." The players love this feeling of freedom, of respect for each one's space. They reject straitjackets, or being labelled as brainless, as if they have no self-will. Mourinho gives them dignity.

This explains the deep trail left by the Portuguese coach wherever he goes. Relationships last over time, even after he's left. John Terry is one of those who stays in touch with José Mourinho to this day:

He went to Italy and then to Spain, but we've kept up a good relationship. We players here at Chelsea even agreed that we wanted to go and see a Real Madrid game and be with José again. He's one of those people you like to keep in touch with. Noone is taking that away from us. **JOHN TERRY**

Mourinho builds solid relationships with brotherhood and… victories. "The victories, especially the historical ones, make these milestones unforgettable, impossible to erase, and bring people even closer together. So it's normal that I have such strong bonds with my players", says José Mourinho.

His old dream is to bring the 'family' together sometime: "It's not possible now because almost all of them are still active, but when I celebrate 25 years of my career I'm going to gather them. It's going to be nice!"

I consider Mourinho to be a very intelligent coach. He knows how to manage his work very well, in a changing room with 25 egos. **PEPE MEL**

"YOU PLAY TOMORROW, I TRUST YOU!"

It had never happened to me before and it's unlikely to ever happen again. I arrived in Milan, on a Friday, 28th of August, coming from Madrid. On the Saturday, the 29th, I was on the field with my new team, Inter. And it wasn't to train or to play a friendly game, no, it was for an important match, one of the most awaited matches of the season: the derby! If I close my eyes and go back to those moments, it's like I'm watching a really intense film, with lots of twists and turns, at an incredible speed. A real thriller!

Real and Inter negotiated for several weeks and meanwhile I moved to Milan. But the situation wasn't solved. There were details to be worked out. I was on living on standby mode. I knew Inter really wanted me, that president Massimo Moratti, the technical director Marco Branca and José Mourinho has chosen me to complete the team, but an agreement had to be reached, a contract signed and the transfer paid. In other words, a casino. Everything was decided that Friday, 28th of August. Only a few hours before negotiations were concluded, I travelled. I left Madrid that Friday and got to Italy quite late. That night, the team was gathered at the Appiano Gentile, Inter's training centre. My new team was already in radio silence, the following day was the game against Milan!

Mourinho had already received a message, a phone call. I knew he wanted me. But I didn't expect what happened next. José greeted me and said: "You play tomorrow. On the team. From the first minute. I trust you, and believe me: you're going to win the derby." I couldn't believe it. I hadn't trained even once with my new partners... I thought: "Shit, this is big, big!"

We won 4-0. A great classic, on Milan soil! To this day I'm stopped by Inter fans on the street to remember that special day. I think I played one of the best games of my career. It was as if I'd always played in Inter and Mourinho had been my coach for many years!

Everything that happened next, everything we won together, is the result of that day. I always said Mourinho has a special place in my heart and in my career. And it all began with a phrase: "You play tomorrow, I trust you."

WESLEY SNEIJDER *

* The only player who made José Mourinho cry in public

COMMUNICATION...

He's like me when I was young. He's got the same enthusiasm. The fans know he's a fighter. For them and for the team.

ALEX FERGUSON

Mourinho sent me messages (of support because of a bad injury) and I'm grateful to him.

SERGIO CANALES

O ne of the first examples of what many would come to call mind games – or Mind Games Master, as the English media prefer to call them – happened on 23rd January, 2002. In a room filled with journalists, at the old Antas stadium, José Mourinho was presented as the new coach for FC Porto. And in a seemingly thoughtless gesture he said: "I'm sure we're going to be champions next year."

The context didn't favour such audacity. The FC Porto team hadn't been champion for two years, was dragging itself through the championship in sixth place, had already kissed the Portugal Cup goodbye – eliminated at home by Sporting de Braga – and Mourinho was the second coach of the season, succeeding Octávio Machado.

It's true that José Mourinho's promise referred to the following season, 2002/03, the one he could put his personal stamp on, by choosing the players and preparing the ground in time. Still, the phrase sounded thoughtless, considering the huge gap between the quality of FC Porto football and winning a title. Mourinho's promise wasn't even the typical, worn out cliché to please the fans. It came straight from the brainbox!

"That phrase was excellent", admits Pinto da Costa. The president of FC Porto had already heard the same thing, minutes before the press conference, when Mourinho approached the players in the changing room: "When he said 'I'm sure we're going to be champions next year', at the same time he said 'this year we'll not be champions'. He showed a great deal of realism and that he wasn't there to cheat anyone. At the same time he took the load off the players. It was like saying, 'forget this year and let's start working for the next season'. He showed determination and faith in what we'd contemplated for the following year."

Rui Faria, who was already a member of the technical team at the time, was scared: "I was 25 years old, to me everything was still new and at that moment I thought we were taking on this challenge in a really heavy way. That meant that we were immediately under pressure to win and to meet our target. If we didn't we'd look ridiculous."

But it was already out. Mourinho had proclaimed it from the top of the platform: "I'm sure we're going to be champions next year." The phrase was swept across all the front pages, it opened every TV news program and filled the radio space. The phenomenon was welcomed with a mix of perplexity, irony and even some mockery from commentators.

'Arrogant' was the first label to come out of certain mouths. Time proved them wrong. The best fitting label was probably 'believer.' When he promised to win the title, Mourinho showed an unbreakable belief, only shared by winners. He simply said what others, faced with the same scenario, would rather hush, thus avoiding exposing themselves and eventually being "ridiculed", as Rui Faria stated.

Mourinho said it, and by saying it he accelerated the rhythm of the Club's Direction, players, fans and even collaborators, as Rui Faria's statement also proves. At the same time he told each and every one of the rivals: "Catch me if you can." Mourinho was trying to get a very napping club's act together.

One year later, precisely halfway through the season promised for the title, Mourinho poked everyone's mind with his words again. One day, annoyed with the constant punishments being given to the FC Porto players, he enters the journalists' room with an ugly face and says: "Under normal conditions we're much better and under normal conditions we're going to be champions. Under abnormal conditions (pause)... we're also going to be champions", punches the table and leaves. The message was given, once again, in and out.

In José Mourinho's career, this kind of warning is recurrent but it's not planned long before. It happens whenever the team needs or their opponents 'ask' for it. You can make many interpretations of what went on over ten years ago, but you can't define operating standards. It is Mourinho's intuition that defines the time and intensity of the shake-up.

THE SPECIAL ONE

José Mourinho arrived at English football with the highest salary of all those who were responsible for training teams: 4.2 million pounds. Besides 'hefty', this figure implied a directly proportional responsibility. Once again, Mourinho wasn't intimidated.

At his Chelsea presentation press conference, in June 2004, the Portuguese manager faced the battalion of flashes with a confident half-smile. And to the array of questions that enclosed a veiled suspicion about his real value, Mourinho didn't mince his words:

"Please don't call me arrogant. It's just that I am the European champion, therefore I think I am a special one." At that moment Mourinho didn't know it, but the expression special one would become eternal in history.

Peter Kenyon, then chief executive of Chelsea, remembers how that was the defining moment for the Portuguese coach: "He raised the bar so very high – even for himself – and put himself under enormous pressure." John Terry, who was team captain at the time, was impressed with his courage and interpreted it as a way of protecting the players: "He put all the pressure on himself and relieved the group of that weight." Perhaps the gesture hadn't been all that calculated, "it was just the reaction of someone who believed in his own qualities, thanks to the passion with which he works", explains Peter Kenyon.

Besides the miles of columns and hundreds of opinions the phrase "I am a special one" triggered, it had another benefit, as Terry explains:

When he arrived, he got all the press attention with the phrase "I am a special one." He knew how to handle the pressure and so he freed the team of that weight. Many coaches who came to England had difficult relationships with the press, but not Mourinho. He was the one who set the rules. **JOHN TERRY**

José Mourinho's relationship with the media was always peaceful. But even when there was some friction, he knew how to come out on top. He won in intelligence and in his unusual speed of thought. For instance, in Italy, when he hot-headedly argued with a journalist about the team he should use for the next game. Annoyed with all the questions, Mourinho turned on the surprise effect: "Let me promise you: you write who the first eleven are going to be and I'll play with your team." Under normal conditions the dialogue would end there, but the other person wasn't conventional and refused to surrender: "If you give part of the nine million you make... even if it's just 500 thousand Euros..." It was a perfect shot and, for the first time, Mourinho seemed to be cornered in the confrontation with a journalist. But in the same breath he reacted, coming out on top: "You're wrong, I make 11 million... 14 with publicity."

When he got to Madrid, José Mourinho knew he'd be faced with the most powerful media he had ever known. Throughout football history, there are quite a number of players and coaches who have been reduced to dust by the Spanish press in no time. Even some of those who were considered untouchable to begin with. In this context, Real Madrid is looked upon as the largest bonfire of all. Mourinho knew of the risks his controversial personality ran in that environment, so he anticipated things. On the day of his presentation, he clarified the issue with one phrase: "I've come here with all my qualities and defects, I am José Mourinho and I'm not going to change."

Soon, everyone realised what a journalistic gem each press conference with Mourinho is and how precious he is to the media's activity. Mourinho sells newspapers, causes clicks on the internet, and raises radio and television audiences. The journalists know it: he's the one who makes the wheel go round.

INTERNAL TARGETS

Communication is also used from the outside in. In his adroit, accurate way, the Portuguese coach often uses the journalists to send messages to his own managers or players. He does so publicly, and deliberately, so that his ideas are recorded for future memory. He likes to use metaphors and adapts his statements to the culture of the countries where he is working, so that the press places greater value on the examples he gives. In Chelsea, when questioned about the team's rotation, he explained with an example of two British cars: "If you have a Bentley and an Aston Martin at home, and if you go out every day with the Bentley and you leave the Aston Martin in the garage, that's stupid." Mourinho was thus rubbing the ego of all the 'Aston Martin's he had in the 'garage'.

Ricardo Carvalho also received a short, direct message from Mourinho when he was complaining about not being in the main eleven in Chelsea: "Ricardo Carvalho seems to have trouble understanding things, maybe he needs to do an IQ test or go to a psychiatric hospital." If this kind of statement were to involve other persons, it would most likely lead to rupture. But not with Mourinho. On the contrary. Not long ago Carvalho confirmed this in an interview for Real Madrid TV: "He says the things he feels and knows how to get the message across. We never resent what he says." Ricardo Carvalho is the player Mourinho brought from FC Porto to Chelsea and later from Chelsea to Real Madrid. The midfielder is none other than the most used player by José Mourinho in his whole career, totalling almost 300 matches.

Does he do it spontaneously, or for show? Maybe both, depending on the situations. Only Mourinho can answer. However, over time, it is possible to identify similar strategies he uses which suggest a pinch of... premeditation. There aren't many examples, but there are a few. In February 2011, in a press conference in Lyon, before a Real Madrid match for the Champions League, the journalists 'harassed' Mourinho to exhaustion about Pedro León not having been summoned to the eleven. He got so fed up that he answered: "I've told you that Benzema is in the eleven and you don't want to know who the other 10 are? If I was you I'd want to know the team." It was the bait for a journalist to put his arm up and ask: "Who are the other ten?" It was the cue for Mourinho to say, "too late now", and leave the room.

Six years earlier, on the eve of a CSKA-Chelsea match for the Champions League, the same old song and dance. Faced with blurred questions, Mourinho rattles the cage: "Don't you want to know who's playing? Fine, if you don't..." Someone asks about the 'eleven', Mourinho says it's too late, laughs out loud and leaves.

José Mourinho doesn't communicate with words only. Mimic has also been in his portfolio several times.

It's almost always directed at the fans – whether opponents or not – and used in a surgical fashion. A gesture that became famous were the three fingers turned towards the San Siro bench, when Real Madrid recently visited Milan for the Champions League, recalling the triplet won when working for Inter. But the most emblematic code of hand signs happened on 6th May 2007, when Chelsea lost all hopes of revalidating the England title. After losing against Arsenal in the Emirates Stadium, the coach greeted practically all the opponents with firm gestures and then looked towards the stand where the Chelsea fans were. With his right-hand palm he pushed his chin up, as if to ask them to leave the stadium as their team would, heads held high. At the same time, with that gesture Mourinho was already beginning to prepare for the England Cup final which was to take place 14 days later. The proof that his gesture had become ingrained in the Blues' pride showed when the players, celebrating their triumph in that final, pushed their chins up with the palms of their hands.

José Mourinho realised, long before anyone else, how important it is to master every form of communication – in words, in gestures and even in writing. That's why, when he left FC Porto, he didn't think twice about accepting the invitation made by the sports paper Record to sign a weekly column for its magazine, Dez. Under the heading "Hotel Chelsea", he began with the one page (the last one of the magazine) and quickly went on to a double page, such was the readers' appetite for the chronicle of the European champions' coach. José Mourinho wrote about everything: a lot about his day-to-day in the English League, but also about Portuguese football and of other championships. His writing was good, direct and objective, and it had soul. Through these texts Mourinho could mark his position in the national football panorama and also send messages to an array of targets.

One of the best examples of this war in writing happened with Johan Cruijff, in October 2005. Mourinho had only been at Chelsea for one season and a few months. Despite having already won the England title, he was still trying to find his place in European football. There were some who wanted to crush the young coach's credibility, thus preventing him from occupying a space that belonged to certain people who were a power in the state. Cruijff was one of those who felt threatened and, during a trip to London, he decided to criticise the Portuguese coach and Chelsea's football. José Mourinho answered on the pages of Dez magazine with a text called "Reply to Cruijff", which would go down in history: "Respecting is certainly not thinking that you own the truth and that others cannot think differently; respecting is certainly not criticising everything and everyone, pen in hand, over the past ten years; respecting is not cheating young students of an almost fictitious course who pay to come and hear you and never

saw you in the flesh; respecting is definitely not using your famous 'entourage' to manipulate opinions; respecting is not coming to England to play golf and fire against someone who is, whether you like it or not, a real professional who has won everything there is to win." As corrosive as acid. For the good of the whole football family, Cruijff was thereby informed about the dangers of playing with this young coach. To top it up, Mourinho also offered some advice to the Dutch coach: "How about teaching us how you won 5-0 against Real Madrid on a memorable night at Camp Nou... and how you suffered 5 in Madrid in another unforgettable classic? Oh yes, that would be a lesson we'd appreciate. I repeat, we have a lot to learn from the experiences of the 'ex', even if those 'ex' haven't won anything we haven't won already."

Two weeks later, Mourinho turned his words into deeds. He eliminated Barcelona in the Champions League eighth-finals, with a clear 4-2 at Stamford Bridge, and he wrote four more lines in Dez magazine: "Johan Cruijff must be thinking why he didn't keep his mouth shut when he said Chelsea didn't play attacking football..."

FIRST, THE GROUP

Usually José Mourinho's more or less controversial public interventions have a single aim: the adamant defence of the group. History proves this. It's an ongoing process. Mourinho is always on duty, in the tiniest gestures, in the most naive reactions and even in statements he seemingly makes out of context.

In April 2006, such a case happened. Chelsea was heading the championship, but Manchester United reduced the difference to seven points. The pressure was growing, and that week the Blues were playing a difficult match. In the press conference before the game, a journalist asked Mourinho if he wasn't worried about his rival's proximity. He answered: "To me, the death of a swan in Scotland because of the bird flu is what disturbs me. I'm more concerned with that situation than with Manchester United. That's been dramatic over the last few days and I'll probably have to go shopping for a mask." This phrase drew laughter from the audience and in the days that followed no-one talked about the game, just about the bird flu. "In the changing room we all thought what a master he was at taking the pressure off the players, it's brilliant", recalls John Terry. Oh, and by the way: Chelsea won the match.

Terry also witnessed another of his leader's shows for the media before the duel of the Champions eighth-finals, between Chelsea and Barcelona, in 2004/05.

Mourinho not only released who his team was, but he also named the 'eleven' that Frank Rijkaard was going to call up. Once again, the element of surprise contributed to destabilise the opponent's balance. Chelsea moved ahead.

In Italy, faced with another critical moment of the season, Mourinho said the words that would even result in merchandising products. Inter was riding towards another title, quite some way ahead, after a match in which it had supposedly been favoured by the referees. The transalpine press devoted that week exclusively to this subject and, as soon as he could, Mourinho flared: "I don't like intellectual prostitution. What I like is intellectual honesty. In these last few days there's been enormous intellectual manipulation. There was a lot of work to talk of nothing but the referees' mistakes in Inter's benefit. No-one talked about a Roma which has great players but will finish the season with zero titles (zero tituli), no-one talked about Milan which has minus 11 points and will finish the season with zero titles (zero tituli), and no-one talked about Juventus which won as many points but with referees' mistakes." The expression zero tituli was so strong that even T-shirts were made with the phrase. Over a year after all this, you could still find these T-shirts for sale near the San Siro stadium.

The Portuguese coach uses this ability to meddle with people's minds like no-one. His gestures are premeditated and valued as if they were a tactical change that decides a game. "On several occasions, I've felt that I changed the opponents' performance with what I say. It doesn't happen always, but it happens often. So I've no doubt that's a road to explore", Mourinho says.

His critics call him arrogant, patronising and disrespectful, whatever the gesture, one way or another. In this regard, it's worth going back to José Mourinho's chronicles in Dez magazine, in 2005, to understand better what he himself thinks of these comments: "The Sunday Guardian had an interesting article about me, which I read with a smile. If Mourinho celebrated with his players and forgot to greet the opponent's coach, like at the end of the match with Blackburn, Mourinho is arrogant in the author's opinion; if in the match with Newcastle the same Mourinho greeted Souness before the final whistle, the scribe's opinion is that Mourinho is arrogant; if in the League Cup final Mourinho crossed 50 metres to greet Benitez and the Liverpool players, Mourinho is arrogant, he insists; and if, while celebrating, he waved to his wife, who was in the stand, he decides that Mourinho provokingly waved to the opposing fans, therefore Mourinho is arrogant. I thank you for the 'journalistic' article, because you made me laugh; I thank you because someone has realised and wanted to realise what I've come to realise a long time ago."

José Mourinho doesn't spare his targets when it involves relentlessly defending his group. With him, the press, the opponents and even his peers run great risks if they step over the line of hypocrisy.

He knows plastic flowers don't smell, wither or die, so he's ruthless with that kind of 'flower'. Sometimes even cruel. Like with Arsène Wenger in England, and then with Cláudio Ranieri in Italy. The thing with the Italian coach had been dragging on since Mourinho replaced him in Chelsea. Ranieri never got over being fired. They met again in Italy – Mourinho in Inter, Ranieri in Roma – and back came the provocations. José Mourinho had enough and hit the Italian veteran in his self-esteem: "I studied Italian six hours a day for several months so as to be able to communicate with my players, with the media and with the fans. Ranieri was in England for five years and all he could say was good morning and good afternoon." The 'Ranieri' episode became even more emblematic when, in 2011 and already as coach of Inter Milan, the 'old' coach dropped the following amazing phrase: "In this club, they should make a statue to Mourinho." A total surrender to the merits of an 'enemy'.

The battle of communication isn't a minor detail. Throughout his career José Mourinho always prepared himself intensively to be able to communicate without restrictions in the language of the countries where he worked. He values this 'weapon', as much as technical or tactical issues. This is the only way he can face the press as their equal: by decoding second intentions in their questions, choosing the right words to answer and surprising them with his prompt reaction. Chelsea and Real Madrid weren't a problem because Mourinho already spoke English and hadn't yet forgotten Spanish from his time in Barcelona. But in Milan it was different. He studied intensively, for months, so as to 'show off' fluent Italian on the day of his presentation in Inter. Once again he caught everyone by surprise. Once again he scored points with the media and gained the warmth of Italian society.

THE PRICE OF WORDS

José Mourinho has already paid dearly for gestures and remarks made throughout his career. Audacity has a price, probably one calculated by the Portuguese coach. The bill will probably enter the section regarding 'expense allowances'. And, after all, you can see how essential it always is for the highly positive balance of each season.

Different football associations (in Portugal, England, Italy and Spain) have given him fines of over 800,000 Euros and 20 games' suspension, in a career of slightly over ten years.

The most famous sanction, because of the consequences it had, was in 2005, when Mourinho was coaching Chelsea. At the end of a match with Barcelona for the Champions League (2-1), at Camp Nou, the Portuguese coach accused the referee, Anders Frisk, and the Barça coach (Frank Rijkaard) of having had a dialogue in the changing room during the break. As a result, the impression was conveyed that this alleged conversation influenced the work of the Swedish referee in the second half, through some very wrong decisions, among them expelling Didier Drogba. The truth is that after this episode Frisk never found peace again – he got countless death threats and was even forced to stop refereeing. The UEFA punished José Mourinho with two matches and a 13,000 euro fine. "Mr. Mourinho must be held accountable for his actions. Perhaps he should analyse what would happen if he did things differently. If he changed, I'm sure he'd have nicer meetings than those he has now", declared the Swedish referee after these incidents.

But Mourinho was never sensitive to this kind of argument. He always understood communication as part of the game. As important as a decisive substitution or an effective tactical system. His opponents – both players, coaches, managers and referees – must be prepared to defend themselves with the same weapons, i.e. words. And when his opponents 'buy' that game, Mourinho seldom loses.

The heaviest fine of his career happened when he was working for Real Madrid. In November 2010, the UEFA gave him five games' suspension – four effective ones and the fifth with a three-year suspended sentence – and a 50,000 euro fine, for misconduct during the Champions League. The most important European football institution considered "inappropriate" José Mourinho's statements after being beaten by Barcelona in the semi-finals, when Pepe was sent off: "I don't know if it's because of UNICEF, I don't know if

it's Ángel María Villar's power (president of the Spanish Football Federation and of the UEFA Arbitration Board). I don't understand. If I say what I think, my career ends here", said Mourinho.

In July 2011, the UEFA Appeals Committee decided to reduce the punishment applied: the same five games' suspension, but only three effective ones and two with a three-year suspended sentence. The 50,000 euro fine was upheld.

INTERRUPTED TRAINING

José Mourinho's relationship with the media is based on an innate ability. The process has surely evolved over time, but looking back it's not hard to identify traits revealing, even then, an expert in the matter.

Let's go back to Mourinho's first experience as head coach. Benfica, October 2000. As usual in every training session, reporters had only 15 minutes to cover the field session. After that, they had to occupy a previously defined place on the stand, all together. They all knew and accepted the rules. Those 15 minutes were valuable and put to good use.

Mourinho understood their difficulties and so he allowed a certain freedom, letting reporters stand around the field instead of confining them to a distant spot with no angle. Until the day the freedom of others invaded his team's work. "We were training and there was one journalist on the field taking pictures", recalls Carlos Mozer, the assistant at the time. "Mourinho stopped the training session, looked at the journalist and said: 'We had an agreement and you're not complying with it. If you don't respect me, I won't respect you either.' And the training was over." The atmosphere became tense. Then, in a calmer manner, he added: "Starting tomorrow, if you comply with what was agreed, everything goes back to normal; if something like today happens, I'll finish the session again."

At that moment, Mourinho sent out two signals: "To the press, showing who made the rules; and to the players, saying he'd do whatever it took to defend them, even stopping a training session", says Mozer.

DON JOSÉ, THE CHRISTOPHER COLUMBUS OF MODERN FOOTBALL

Three strokes of luck, connected to one another and all at once. A fate to which I honestly have to say — thank you! Working for Massimo Maratti's Inter since February 2003 gave me the chance to participate in the Nerazzurra experience of José Mourinho, thus going through the legendary 2009/10 season (and not just as a fan), which resulted in the prodigious conquest of the Scudetto, the Italy Cup and the Champions League.

I'm one lucky communications manager and press officer! I'm aware of that and I will always be grateful to all those who allowed me to contribute to some extent to everything that happened and will never be forgotten.

I picked up Mourinho for the first time on my 'curiosity radar' after he won the Champions League with FC Porto. He won the most important cup with a team no-one expected to win, and he didn't join in the party: head held high and with a tough smile, he suddenly left the field. Sitting in front of the telly, I said: "This one's the greatest". Only on two other occasions did I have a similar feeling: when I saw young Ronaldo play for PSV Eindhoven, and when I watched the joyous leap to fame of the young Uruguayan Alvaro Recoba who, during one of Inter's friendly matches, came onto the pitch to occupy the place of the Brazilian phenomenon, and the first time he touched the ball he kicked it from midfield and hit the post.

It's in the spring of 2008, with Mourinho's arrival at Inter, that I become certain of what I'd inferred from TV. I must admit that, at the time, I was evaluating another professional opportunity, not because I felt dissatisfied with my internal role in the Nerazzurro club, but because of my adventurous spirit, in search of new worlds and new emotions. When I heard José Mourinho was coming, I immediately put my doubts aside: "I want to try this before anything else." I hadn't yet met Don José personally. I'd seen him over and over again on TV with Chelsea, read and re-read things about him, but now that he was arriving he was very real, direct and unique. I couldn't miss him.

Indeed, a few days later, president Massimo Moratti told me: "With Mourinho we're going to achieve something new and unique." True. As always, Massimo Moratti anticipated what would happen. To all of us, Don José was the discovery of a whole different world, our Christopher Columbus of modern football. And I'm not writing this just because this book is dedicated to him. It's the historical, objective truth.

I also had big discussions with Mourinho. For a while, for a couple of months at the start of 2010, we weren't even on speaking terms. Maybe it was my fault, maybe someone played the wise guy and managed to get us against each other. It doesn't matter. Now everything's over because in the end we sorted things out. And nowadays, even more than before, to me Don José is above all a magnificent person, unique in his own way. He's difficult, never ever banal, but honest and forthright.

Mourinho revolutionised communication for coaches in Italy and in the whole world and history will remember this.

One day we'll explain to our grandchildren the 'before' and the 'after' Mourinho. But right now I'd like to set something straight, that's really important to me: Don José isn't a fantastic communicator as he's made out to be, or to be labelled and sold as a disposable item in the 'throw away' mentality. Don José is, first and foremost, an excellent coach and man. A tireless professional, an expert in tactics, a general who lives within his army and stuns everyone by setting the example. Mourinho doesn't lead a team during a game, he plays with the team, he's on the pitch, he's the epicentre of a victory and of a defeat.

Don José is a strange form of love: either you're with him, or against him. He'll never be the majority's apple of the eye as public opinion goes, but no-one will be indifferent to him either. In his relationship with journalists he's a coach. He prepares himself, he wants to understand, he leaves nothing to chance, he also plays the communication game with self-control, with no fears and with the humility of the great. He uses his intelligence first, so he's not into many schemes. He confronts him-self, assesses the advice he's given, has the ability to make you the protagonist and not just the manager of a club taking care of the media. With respect to communication, Mourinho has the same freedom he's conquered on the pitch. He can say what he thinks, even if he's wrong – and sometimes he is – because he has no limits. His football is global, it's not just about the Portuguese, English, Italian or Spanish 'periphery'. He doesn't say this or that to gain something. He doesn't look for allies, it's always the others who hope to become his allies.

Every morning with Mourinho in Inter, I'd say to myself: "What's he going to make up today?" Morning, day, night. Meetings, phone calls, text messages. A motor that never turns off. The first to arrive, the last to leave. Emotional, exciting, solitary, consensual, black and blue. Fantastic! I'll never forget the privilege of having participated in an Italian broadcast, which wasn't even about sports: "Chiambretti Night." All that I did for him on that occasion doesn't compare to his capacity to remain on stage and win a showdown with the host, Piero Chiambretti, who got all his guests in trouble, except for Don José. On that occasion, Mourinho could be compared to Diego Milito at the end of the Madrid Champions between Inter and Bayern Munich: he was a ruthless bomber who didn't miss a single ball, a single phrase, a single mention. Always the actor, only of himself, without a single memorised part, he himself owns an infinite memory, knowledge and taste for study. He systematises a lot, but never misses the details. With improvised phrases, as if carved into stone when he says "non sono un pirla", "zero tituli", polished, articulated, gesticulated explanations… with sincerity.

His voice and his eyes. Two natural gifts that are striking for many of Mourinho's experts. A deep voice, in all languages (or many) of the world. Eyes that make his interlocutors drop their guard, that catch their attention, that are blunt as a punch in the stomach or as a caress on your cheek. All he taught me wasn't offered in vain. Especially the thing about "Don Paolo", which still makes me very emotional whenever I remember.

PAOLO VIGANÒ *

* Communication Manager of F.C. Internazionale

FORTHRIGHTNESS...

Mourinho says what he has to say, and that's that. You never resent what he says because he respects our way of thinking.

RICARDO CARVALHO

Real Madrid needed someone like Mourinho, a reference with his character and personality. Every day I am learning with him. He pays attention to everything and is always helping us improve.

SERGIO RAMOS

n February 2011, the Portuguese bank Millennium BCP gathered its staff in the Atlantic Pavilion, in Lisbon, to announce its new ambassador. They chose José Mourinho as the face of their brand. With him the bank intends to "promote, generate value and increase its prestige."

Mourinho wasn't present at the session, but he sent an encouragement video, an adapted version of the advertising spot that would 'flood' Portuguese TVs days later:

"(…) I'm not the best, but no-one's better than I am. I simply put my heart and soul into what I do. That's what we have in common. (…) We share the same spirit of victory and we're always there to win, me on the pitch, you in your workplaces. (…) Because our work is our passion."

About 6,500 workers heard and applauded these words. The most heard compliment among the staff members at the venue was… 'forthrightness'. The forthrightness with which José Mourinho said what many of them would have probably liked to have already said; his capacity to convince others with frank, direct arguments; the need to communicate eye to eye, head-on, bluntly.

The tone and manner used to address the collar-and-tie workers at the Atlantic Pavilion are the same Mourinho uses in his daily relationship with the players. "I worked with him for two and a half years and from day one I could tell he was someone different. In terms of his speech, but also in the way he looked into the eyes of the players, in the way he believed in what he said. Sometimes coaches make speeches to intimidate, but they don't believe in what they're saying. He does", says Costinha.

Didier Drogba reaffirms that "Mourinho's eyes never lie and are never warped by anything".

He's special because, in the first place, he'll always tell the truth. Even if you have a personal relationship with him off the pitch, even if you communicate well with him… on the pitch it's work, it's seriousness, it's concentration. **DIDIER DROGBA**

This commitment to the truth, sincerity and forthrightness doesn't choose names or status. Mourinho doesn't look at who you are before a conversation, however delicate it might be: "He looks his players in the eye. Whatever he has to say, he says it, regardless of who it is. He doesn't say things behind your back, he says them to your face… whoever the player is", ensures Silvino Louro, goalkeeper coach.

Jorge Costa goes back to the time when Mourinho was still Bobby Robson's number two in FC Porto. "As assistant coach he was similar to what he was later as head coach: fun, playful, but also very outspoken in his relationships.

This feature improved when he took the leading role. It was something we weren't used to in the player-coach relationship. The chance to question everything, to have open talks about football or even about other topics. He was outspoken, but at the same time he demanded the same from us."

The main difference I noticed from the start was his forthrightness. It wasn't normal for the players to have that transparency and ease to question things, to have an open talk about football or other topics. **JORGE COSTA**

The Portuguese coach's forthrightness leaves no room for mistakes or misunderstandings. "No player can complain about lack of information or about not knowing what plans are defined for him" – says Costinha – "even if those plans are unpleasant for the player in question. For example, he actually said to some players' face, 'I'm not counting on you this season', and then he'd explain his reasons for making those decisions. If that player stayed on in the club, Zé would treat him just like he treated all the others, but the player already knew he wasn't part of the picture. That helped because at that moment, probably his agent was out looking for an immediate solution. So the players had no chance of saying later than no-one had warned them or that they'd been misled. Even in this he anticipates timings."

CALL A SPADE A SPADE

It's with his forthrightness that José Mourinho manages to keep a group of 23 or 24 players motivated, especially those who aren't on the squad. "He's special because he's open. He'll tell you what he thinks anytime. He'll tell you what his intentions are

regarding a certain player. When he takes you off the team, he always tells you why.

He keeps everyone motivated, which isn't easy. In a big club it's even harder because you've got over 20 players, all top quality, who therefore have legitimate expectations of playing. The truth is, when you're playing in a club the size of Chelsea, it's impossible to play in all the games because the season is long. Choices have to be made and José makes them and always justifies them, face to face, with valid reasons", says Petr Cech.

Mourinho demands to be 'paid back' the same way: "He's a coach who won't stand for lies, he's a coach who won't take being stabbed in the back, he's a coach who accepts direct criticism. He handles direct criticism well. He reacts badly when he's criticised outside the four walls of the changing room. Whoever respects these rules will have all he wants from him, because he makes himself available to help", explains Costinha.

He says everything to your face and if you do what he wants you've got your opportunity. He's a very demanding coach, but above all he's intelligent and thoughtful. **VARANE**

With Mourinho, the way to handle problems is identical to that of any worthy family, "he puts the athlete completely at ease and I think he even puts the management at ease." Recently, Mourinho had an attitude that confirms Costinha's assumption. Halfway through the 2010/11 season, the Spanish press disclosed rumours about Mourinho being very likely to exit Real Madrid due to alleged differences with the structure of the club. At the earliest opportunity, the journalists interrogated the coach about the matter and Mourinho was very clear: "There is no ideal situation, but I adapt to any model where there's forthrightness, empathy and in which the coach is only a coach, with his competences. I don't want to have more competences, I just want to be coach." Forthrightness is an omnipresent word in José Mourinho's speech and actions.

The Portuguese coach has stuck to this principle from the first moment he put on the armband of head coach. It's been written, spoken and demonstrated at every moment of his career over these 11 years. No-one can say they don't know the rules. It's called coherence, and it's what Rui Faria considers to be José Mourinho's greatest virtue:

He's just... himself. Every single day. He's coherent in his relationship with people and in everything he does. His coherence shows in his capacity for leadership, for management, for training, for getting the best out of the human resources around him. Coherence is his strongest feature, and it makes him the coach that he is. **RUI FARIA**

Commenting a five-game punishment applied to Alex Ferguson for criticising some refereeing in the Premier League, the Manchester United coach said: "Football is the only industry where you can't say the truth." Mourinho can also talk about that from his own experience. Forthrightness collides head-on with the dominant principle in football that 'what's true today will be a lie tomorrow.'

IN TRAINING...

Every day I learn with him. He pays attention to everything and that helps you improve all the time.

SERGIO RAMOS

After a match with Villarreal, Mourinho sat down next to me and asked me what I intended to do. He said he liked me very much, but he'd understand and even help me if I wanted to leave. Mourinho's words were decisive, because if he'd told me he wasn't interested in my staying on, I'd be lost.

KAKÁ

J osé Mourinho's relationship to training was one of the factors that caused great uproar in traditional football. Those who were more lenient found it strange, while others described it in a far more bizarre way.

Mourinho presented himself without a physical trainer, which was something many found unacceptable. The concept of physical training was not in his books. He had no folders with exercises for strength, speed or resistance. There were no numbers regarding task duration, intensity or repetition. But there was a novel association between the physical dimension and the rest of the training, an integrated behaviour. That's why one of the most important books for José Mourinho, but in the negative, is Lév Matvéiev's 'bible' for physical education and sports students. Obsessed with methodology, this Russian teacher invented, in the late 1950s, the periodisation of training, defending the transfer of physical training from individual sports to collective sports.

José Mourinho's training shows exactly the opposite of this theory. It serves to practise the principles of game and to adapt the players to common ideas. Its great objective is to establish the same behavioural language. From this point onwards, it's all practical, objective and pragmatic: only the situations that matter most are dealt with, depending on the recovery for the game, the progressiveness and the alternation. This integration of objectives requires the assistants' constant intervention. Rui Faria and Silvino Louro are the most active ones (after all, this defines their respective functions), but José Mourinho likes to have all his collaborators on the pitch, including José Morais, the man who prepares reports on the opponents. Any information may prove valuable to tune up the machine.

While others were obsessed with exercise times, rest, repetitions and so on, Mourinho preferred to use his brains to suit the exercises to the principles of game. And how? With a lot of imagination and work. Quality over quantity.

Pinto da Costa followed the training habits of all the coaches who worked for FC Porto. There were 17 of them, from Pedroto to André Villas-Boas, Artur Jorge, António Oliveira or Jesualdo Ferreira. The methodology he most liked was Bobby Robson's, whose assistant was precisely José Mourinho: "Robson made the training sessions really lively, he'd go to the midst of the players, correct them, motivate them, and I think Mourinho inherited that way of instilling in players the idea that training is as much a competition as playing. With Mourinho, the players know that only those who do better in training will play, and that motivates them. Mourinho actually improved Robson's methodology even more, by making it more dynamic and with a greater participation of the players. That was crucial for the success of FC Porto."

The most important symptom of the efficacy of his methods is worded by his athletes: "I often say that I don't know one single player who badmouths his training, not even those who aren't playing. That shows his quality as coach and manager of a group", says Costinha.

Didier Drogba worked long enough with José Mourinho to be able to confirm Costinha's theory: "Working with him was really fantastic!"

For three and a half, four years, the training sessions were different every day. It was always a pleasure to train. I always learned something with him every day. **DIDIER DROGBA**

"José developed my tactical intelligence hugely", the Ivory Coast attacker stressed.

Training is so welcome by the athletes that Mourinho doesn't need to raise his voice: "He doesn't make a player work hard because the training sessions are so good that the players work spontaneously and do what he wants", adds Costinha. It's the best stimulus to get out of bed, says Maniche: "I'd get up in the morning with a smile because I knew training was always good."

There's something essential to keep up the levels of motivation. John Terry explains what it is: "All he did during the training included a ball. Even in the pre-season, which is a stage where you usually run, run, run, but not with him. There was a ball from day one. And we enjoyed it."

EXERCISES WITH A LIFE OF THEIR OWN

Mourinho is the first to arrive at the training centre. He reads a summary of the daily papers, prepared for him by the press officer, answers emails in his mobile phone and goes off to the field. He's up early because he doesn't tolerate logistic or procedural flaws in the training sessions. Each session has to be one hundred percent profitable for the players.

There is no generic prescription for training. José Mourinho defines it according to the team's objectives, to the opponent and to the athletes' physical condition. That's why there are no two equal training sessions. Mourinho builds sessions à la carte which allow him to get exactly what he wants from the team. The best witness to confirm this method is Rui Faria: "In training he has qualities that allow him to objectively choose what he wants to do. Nowadays, in terms of high performance, that's a very difficult task. There are many games and little time to train. Knowing how to choose what to do in training is fundamental and Mourinho has that insight. He knows how to find the best exercise to fulfil the objectives he has set out for the next match. He is definitely the best", guarantees his assistant coach.

Simple, direct communication also helps. "It's a great advantage he has over many other coaches: some coaches I know need a lifetime to explain something, but with Zé, he just has to say it once and the players understand him straight away. He uses the so-called football jargon, based on simple, direct terms. Everyone gets it", explains Silvino Louro, the goalkeeper coach.

The same exercise in the hands of different people produces different results. Each coach has his own way of conducting a task. In this field of expertise, Mourinho is a few steps ahead of the others: "He gives the exercises a life of their own, gives them soul. And he manages that because he knows perfectly well what he wants with that exercise and during the exercise what he wants from each player. That's why he often changes the initial scheme, arranging it so that it translates his ideas", explains Rui Faria. "I would say that his organisational skills, his capacity to choose what's really essential, his perception of what the team's needs actually are, and his capacity to do this on the pitch, make him a different coach."

Many times, what we do in an hour and a half of training, other coaches probably can't do in two hours. **RUI FARIA**

Each training session is an authentic lab where you can even clone opponents. When the intention is to refine a certain type of strategy, depending on the specific characteristics of an opponent, Mourinho asks for the direct intervention of the players who will not be in the eleven. He organises a team with a profile identical to that of the opponent and asks each of the athletes to behave similarly to the rival. According to this, he works with the main team on game situations very close to reality. "With this method, he explains in practice what the opponent's strong points and weak points are. It's not just any explanation, it's one based on a visual and practical image, which is extremely important for players to grasp", says Rui Faria.

José Mourinho takes the training as far as possible. He anticipates scenarios, even the most unlikely ones. The last example of this happened in the 2010/11 season, against Espanyol. Iker Casillas was sent off two minutes after the match began. Real Madrid played for over 90 minutes outnumbered. It would have been panic for a lot of teams, but not for Mourinho's. Pepe explains why: "When we were left with 10 players we knew what we had to do, because Mourinho massacred us to train for these situations. When Iker was sent off, Mourinho told us to apply a tactic we'd rehearsed in training. We closed up in a sort of pyramid and they were forced to play outwards, they'd pass the ball back and do diagonals", reveals the central defender for Real Madrid.

JOY AT WORK

Smiles and laughter aren't left outside by the training door. Mourinho himself invites them in, but it's the coach who defines how and when. "He knows the perfect timing to play and to work", declares Costinha. John Terry confirms this: "One of the things he demanded was that players know how to separate fun time and work time. When it was time to play, we all did, a lot."

When we had to work, we all worked hard. Always. It was a point of honour for him. No-one dared mess about at a serious moment. **JOHN TERRY**

When the moment is to relax, Mourinho's the most enthusiastic of all. "Often in training we'd do circles of eight against two. He'd come up, pull his tracksuit trousers up and start tackling. It was playful, but at the same time he wanted to show us his competitive state of mind. We had a lot of fun with him", Didier Drogba tells us. "José liked to have fun. Him, Rui Faria, Silvino and Baltemar Brito were a group of good people. They created a fantastic atmosphere and that made us really enjoy the training sessions", stresses John Terry.

The same man who opens the window of good humour is the same one who closes it to round up. Sometimes, Mourinho needs to shake people up. But he does so logically, constructively and coherently: "We were playing a casual match, five versus five, and after a few minutes the result was already 5-4. He stopped the game, completely furious with the players, and said: 'How is it possible that in a five versus five game, after half a dozen minutes, the result is 5-4? It's impossible! It's got to be 1-0 or 1-1. If you don't know how to defend you're not doing your job. It's five versus five, it's easier to defend. That means you're not defending, you're not doing your job!' We were all very surprised. It was the first time we heard something of the kind. The truth is, his arguments made sense. As goalkeeper, I don't want to let goals in. Well, a 5-4 score isn't really a positive score for the goalkeeper or for a defence", recalls Petr Cech.

Individual conversations during training aren't very common, but when they do happen Mourinho prefers to talk in the player's native tongue so there is no noise in their communication. The language chosen for the group lectures is always that of the country where he is training, as an example of respect for the club's patriotic values.

DRINKING WATER AGAINST THE CLOCK

The stopwatch is a fundamental gadget in José Mourinho's training sessions. With it, he keeps up the intensity and ensures sessions are fully profitable. Everything is measured to the second, so as not to waste time. Even drinking water moments are timed. Mozer, assistant to Mourinho in his first experience as head coach, remembers an emblematic episode: "Zé gave players a one-minute pause to drink water. And he'd warn them in a firm voice: 'One minute!' The players had other habits and they suffered a bit at the beginning. Instead of drinking water quickly, they would chat calmly. When the time was up, Zé whistled. Some of them signalled to explain they hadn't drunk yet and he replied: 'Too bad! Next time drink faster!' In fact after two or three training sessions everyone drank in silence and within the minute allowed."

Training is sacred for José Mourinho. It has moments of maximum demand. On several occasions he broke up a casual game going on between players because they weren't making enough of an effort. Maniche remembers one particular episode, when both were in FC Porto: "We had a lot of team lunches, which was one of the ways to build our group spirit."

One day we went training after one of those lunches. But during that session there just wasn't that eagerness to work... he realised this and ended the session in five minutes. **MANICHE**

When Mourinho realises the training session isn't going to yield the intended results, he prefers not to waste time. He doesn't train his players to respect a timetable or to make believe.

VALUABLE LESSONS FOR THE FUTURE

I clearly remember my first meeting with José Mourinho, in 2004. I was a member of the technical staff in Chelsea, I'd worked with Claudio Ranieri, and I received a phone call to go to Stamford Bridge to meet the new manager. I confess I didn't know what to expect of that meeting because although he'd just won the Champions with FC Porto, his name was nothing special. Regarding my future, I had even bigger doubts. When you meet a new manager and you have an interview set up with him, there are only two possibilities: either you leave the interview still with a job, or you leave it unemployed. Honestly, I didn't know whether he wanted to keep me on or send me away.

Fortunately I stayed and I'm glad I did. Those were memorable years for me. The best compliment I can make about José is to say that, during the time we worked together, I changed completely. I changed because I learned more with him than with all the other coaches with whom I'd worked before. I learned and embraced much of his philosophy and of his working methods. Having worked with Mourinho gave me the opportunity to improve my own performance as coach and to draw many learnings from his exercises and from his methods. That allowed me to progress as a professional. This is probably the best tribute I can pay him.

There were a lot of differences between José Mourinho and the previous coach, Ranieri. Different methodologies. Ranieri had more 'Italian' methods, meaning that the tactical part of training was separated from the physical part. When José arrived, he began to teach these elements together and the players responded extremely well to this novelty.

Mourinho included a ball in every exercise and the players loved that. As the exercises were all very physical, if you include a ball, the athletes tolerate them better. That's what happened.

'Intensity' was a key word in work. José Mourinho got the players to understand how important daily training was. He made them see that all the sessions were important, that each and every exercise was

important. He brought intensity to the training activity and even to the club itself. He knew how to transmit this to the players, who then transported this attitude to the games.

For him, training was serious and totally professional. The time to laugh and play around was always outside work, outside football. This feature was more noticeable in the first season. Mourinho was very demanding – deliberately demanding, I would say – with the players during the sessions, to make sure that every day they'd work to their fullest capacity. It was a way of taking a stand and making it clear that, with him, that's how it would be.

He'd say insistently, "Give me more, give me more". But it's also true that when the players gave their best he was there to support them. Mourinho liked to support the people who worked for him. He's extremely demanding, but he's there to help if you have a problem, or if you're fighting against something, whatever it may be. You know he'll be by your side.

The day I said goodbye to him was hard. The one thing you know for sure when you start working as a coach or manager is that one day it will come to an end. But in the case of José Mourinho I think his farewell to Chelsea happened too soon. Everyone felt that. Fortunately I developed a good relationship with him, as well as with the players, and that gave me the confidence to move on as a coach.

Working with Mourinho gave me other opportunities, in other clubs, which was great for me and for my career.

To this day I still use some of the exercises we did in Chelsea, adapting them to other clubs and other circumstances. A coach who watches Mourinho's good ideas learns how to develop them and use them in other ways.

We still talk, not every day, but regularly during the season, whether it's about certain games, certain players, or about our families and so on. So, my message to José is that he keeps up his good work and I thank him for the help he gave me in my career. One day I hope to be again a member of one of his technical teams.

STEVE CLARK *

---

* In June 2004, Steve Clark was invited by José Mourinho - who had just been hired as Chelsea manager - to integrate the Blues' main technical team. So Clark left the youth section of the London club and became one of Mourinho's right-hand men, taking on a role as privileged witness of the work developed by the Portuguese coach. His professional relationship with the Special One ended only in September 2007, when Mourinho left the head of the team.

IN THE GAME...

Mourinho's Real Madrid is one of the best teams I've seen playing.

ALFREDO DI STÉFANO

Conclusions are drawn from each Real Madrid match and that's how you see that Mourinho is the best.

MARADONA

I f someone shows such good results in various teams, as happens with José Mourinho, it's because he's got to be a great psychologist and a great strategist. Every decision, whether in a context of football, chess, military or politics, stems from the same principle. You must have a good understanding of the nature of the problems to be able to gather elements and develop a strategy."

Gary Kasparov, the best chess player ever and youngest champion (at just 22 years of age) in his domain, knows what he's talking about. Now retired, Kasparov compares Mourinho to the most skilled of strategists.

The most remote origin of the word strategy comes from the ancient Greek stratègós, whose definition fits Mourinho like a glove: "The art of the general."

The game is the final consequence of the strategy. There, the Portuguese coach takes on the level of Master. He handles the pieces with unusual dexterity and speed of thought. He intervenes on the board (pitch) as if he were inside it, making decisions that materialise directly in goals or in the best way to avoid them.

When they step onto the pitch, Mourinho's players know exactly what to do when faced with different situations, both if they have been predicted or not. "He won't have to explain anything, because we've already been trained for everything. When we enter the pitch we're sure of our tasks and we believe in our work", explains Didier Drogba.

The rest is dictated by the circumstances of the game. To a coach, those 90 minutes are about the capacity to see better, faster and make the wisest decision. Space and time are decisive. Timing is essential. On the bench, Mourinho watches every detail, even when he seems to be emotionally out of control: "Whenever necessary, he has the capacity to transmit an expression of stress, of pressure, of demand... but at the same time he's calm inside, capable of analysing all that's going on. This has to do with emotional intelligence", explains assistant Rui Faria. "Behaviourally, he can express a certain kind of demand, aggressiveness, tension, but at the same time he can be very serene in his analyses, in his observations. It seems paradoxical, but it reveals a lot of what he is. He places himself on a different behavioural level according to the needs of the group." This 'two in one' gives him an edge over his rivals regarding the speed with which decisions have to be made. While others need tight time compartments – to switch off rationality and switch on emotional lack of control; to switch off emotional lack of control and switch on rationality -, Mourinho accomplishes both processes at the same time.

What's difficult is to guarantee that José Mourinho actually loses his emotional control on the bench. When he kicks a bottle or makes broad gestures in the face of the fourth referee, the Portuguese coach is still aware of his actions. Rui Faria has already watched dozens of scenes of this kind and he suspects Mourinho's control is absolute: "I think it's all done in a very intelligent manner. Obviously those moments express his emotions at a given moment, but they never represent a lack of control regarding his balance. His fury is the result of a certain displeasure and, in fact, this expression of displeasure is very typical of his personality, but he's always perfectly aware of everything."

Mourinho is the twelfth player of the team. He lives incidents intensely and has even got to the point of stepping onto the pitch. This happened in the 2002/03 season, when FC Porto played the UEFA Cup semi-final against Lazio, in the Antas stadium. Mourinho also 'played' in that game: "Everything happened next to our bench, when a Lazio player, Castroman, was preparing a quick throw-in from the touch line, taking advantage of a counter-attack situation and thus trying to catch our defence off guard. At that moment, Mourinho decided to lightly kick the ball, which was enough to prevent the quick throw-in from the touch line and to allow our team to reorganise its defence", recalls Rui Faria. It was the last minute of the match, FC Porto was winning 4-1, and a possible goal by Lazio at that point could threaten the second leg match. In fact it would allow Lazio to eliminate FC Porto with a score of 2-0 in Rome.

José Mourinho's 'mischief' got him expelled, a one-game punishment imposed by UEFA and a two thousand euro fine. However, this was a small price to pay compared to the profit achieved: that gesture might have prevented a goal and, ultimately, contributed to the presence of FC Porto in the UEFA Cup final. But above all it showed something else: "Only someone who is also playing can do that. Put into context, these are moments that say a lot about the type of personality and character that he transmits to the players", the assistant coach says.

CLEVER MOVES

José Mourinho never scored a goal from the bench. It's against the rules of the game. But he has contributed decisively to a large number of them through good decisions. The moment we can perhaps more accurately state that Mourinho 'scored', happened during a match between Milan and Inter, for the Italian Championship, in 2010. The Interistas were winning 1-0, but they were playing with 10 players only. A win wasn't guaranteed. The Portuguese coach chose to make a replacement, but he retreated immediately, and with this interruption he 'scored' 2-0.

I was about to replace Pandev. At that precise moment a free kick was awarded to our team, near their area. I ran to the fourth referee to postpone the replacement. Pandev stayed on the pitch a minute longer, took that free kick and scored the goal. The free kick foul had been committed in the same place where we'd rehearsed over and over again during that week. **JOSÉ MOURINHO**

The players called him a "sorcerer", Mourinho shrugs his shoulders and says he just joined the dots. "In that case it wasn't going to make a difference if I replaced him now or in one minute. If the game offered us the opportunity to do a move which Pandev had trained so many times, I thought, let's see if it works out. And it did." His reasoning was logical but cold, simple but resorting to memory. The euphoria was still high when Mourinho, smiling, said to the bench: "This goal's mine!" The truth is the Portuguese coach won his last derby in Milan this way.

Three years earlier, in England, Paulo Ferreira had also scored a goal with Mourinho's head. Before a match for the England Cup, the Portuguese player was surprised with the coach's approach: "Paulo, today you're going to the corners." It was unheard of until then.

Paulo Ferreira never had orders to go up to the opponent's area. But on that day Mourinho really insisted with his full-back.

"I don't want you to jump or divide with anyone, I just want you to get near the second post and wait for the ball which is going to come to that zone. You'll see how you'll score." In fact I went up with the first corner, the ball fell at the second post - just as he'd said - and I scored. **PAULO FERREIRA**

One finger up, a wink of the eye or a slight head shake are what it takes for José Mourinho to communicate with his players on the pitch. "Often you just had to look at him, you just had to see the way he was gesturing and you immediately understood what he wanted", says Costinha.

In Spain, Mourinho chooses to put his hand in front of his mouth every time he talks to players or assistants during the game. The Portuguese coach realised that Spanish TV broadcasters have exclusive cameras turned to him during the 90 minutes, to then explore lip reading exhaustively. By covering his mouth, Mourinho avoids exposing publicly messages that are private.

During the match, a gesture can also be used as a (deliberate) communication flaw. This happened in the last round of 2008/09, the first season he coached Inter Milan, against Atalanta. The Nerazzurri were practically champions already, but Ibrahimovic was still fighting for the Calcio top scorer title. He needed one goal to win the trophy. "I remember that on a personal call, Balotteli, instead of passing the ball to Ibra, who was well placed, shot at the goal himself", recalls Rui Faria. "The Swede's immediate reaction was to ask to be replaced. He requested it several times. It seemed an immature way to behave and maybe with another coach it might have resulted in an immediate replacement and subsequent punishment.

On the bench, Zé made it abundantly clear that he didn't understand what the player was requesting. Then he came in our direction and said: 'Look at this guy, what does he want?' When Ibrahimovic approached the bench to put into words what he'd repeated so many times in gestures, Zé told him: 'You want water, is that it?' And he threw him a bottle. He ignored his pleas Once more. Ibrahimovic was confused and a short while later, in the 81st minute, he scored the goal he needed to become the best scorer of the Italian championship", concludes assistant Rui Faria.

With Didier Drogba the intervention was more direct: "At the end of the FA Cup against Manchester United, we were tied 0-0 in extra time. I said to him: 'I'm tired, I can't take it anymore!' He replied: 'No, no, no! Keep going! You're going to score real soon, you'll see!' I stayed focused and during one of the following moves, I scored. That's why at the end of the game I ran over to him to give him a hug", says Drogba.

HALF-TIME SHOW

José Mourinho always enters the field with a notebook and a pen in his coat pocket. It's with these two gadgets that he prepares half-time: "I've got to interpret the game and transform it into feedback for my players. I jot things down and decode the most relevant things that happened during the first half. Half-time is just a ten-minute break during which you often do nothing, you often decide nothing, and which is usually not important. But sometimes half-time can make a difference", explains Mourinho.

And it has made a difference, many times. Diego Milito remembers one such important half-time. Inter was losing 1-0 in Cagliari. The Argentine's performance was basically low. Mourinho entered the changing room with his eyes on Milito and ended up shattering his ego.

He totally thrashed me and really pushed my buttons. In the second half I scored twice and we won. He knows exactly when to press or release a player. **DIEGO MILITO**

Milito scored in the 51st and 55th minutes, that is, six and ten minutes after having listened to José Mourinho's words.

Marco Materazzi was often a substitute in Inter Milan. Therefore he was more available to observe the coach chiding his mates: "He spared no-one. When he had to say something he was always really hard. And he did it in that unique way of his to fluster our pride."

Jorge Costa also watched many such moments. Today, as a coach, he values the methods used by Mourinho even more: "It's really difficult, at a bad moment, for a coach to have the wisdom to not raise the level of his voice and to manage to correct mistakes calmly. But then, in identical circumstances, to change his strategy completely, get to the changing room and kick a bottle or a bag. One way or the other he always managed to get at us and at the same time correct what was wrong. Getting at a player isn't that hard actually, what's hard is to have the capacity, at the same time, to correct what's wrong. Nowadays, as a coach, I can assure you it's really very hard."

The match considered by many to be the key to Inter winning the 2009/10 Champions League, against Dynamo Kiev in the groups phase, was decided like that – at half-time. Zanetti, the captain, tells us how they turned around the 1-0 result in Ukraine: "That drawback could drive us away from the eighth-finals. We needed to win. I clearly remember José's talk during half-time. He appealed to our emotion and our pride so deeply that everyone was touched." Milito and Sneijder turned the game around in the last ten minutes.

The description of Inter's second half can be read in newspaper articles. Words such as 'maturity', 'determination', 'ambition' and 'clarity' are present in most of them. Inter was in second place in Group F. Then it eliminated Chelsea, CSKA and Barcelona (in a historical duel), before defeating Bayern Munich at the final in Madrid.

SOLITARY DECISIONS

José Mourinho doesn't exclude others' opinions from his decisions, but he doesn't look upon such opinions as being crucial. Rui Faria, who has occupied the seat next to his on the substitutes' bench hundreds of times, guarantees that Mourinho is solitary when it comes to making decisions: "He's a person with very clear ideas.

On the bench he might actually ask for opinions, but he's already got a clear idea of what he's going to do. He asks for opinions to check if he's missed something, if someone can add any idea to his. But usually what he wants to do is very clear in his mind."

Several things justify this solitary process. One of the most striking ones is other people's incapacity to keep pace with Mourinho's courage on the bench. "Over these 11 years I've seen us win many games with decisions made by the coach. Decisions of pure risk. He's aware of that and he's prepared for it, it's true, but they're still a risk. He has no fear! He goes ahead and firmly believes in the efficacy of his decisions, as dangerous as they may be. He prefers to run the risk while he can, than to get to the end of the game and be sorry for what he could have done and didn't do", explains Rui Faria.

One special game happened in San Siro for the Italian championship, in the 2009/10 season, against Siena. The match was truly schizophrenic, the score hopping around until it hit 1-2 in favour of the visiting team. Inter's last minutes in search of a draw were suffocating. Mourinho made midfielder Walter Samuel move up to striker position. And then in the 88th minute Sneijder scores the equalising goal. The Nerazzurri nation celebrated that draw as if it were a win. Not Mourinho, though: "After the goal, right on top of the 90th minute, Samuel started asking if he could go back to his position as midfielder. Mourinho gave him a shout that I think was heard even outside the stadium: 'No! Stay there! Stay there!' It seemed like he wasn't thinking straight. Given the circumstances, a draw was great. So it was, but Samuel stayed as striker and scored the winning goal (3-2) in the 93rd minute."

Bernd Schuster, the great German talent who played for Barcelona and for Real Madrid, and was champion in the Merengue club as coach, made an interesting analogy: "I compare Mourinho to John McEnroe, who needed to become irritated to play better." True, to some extent. Mourinho feels comfortable on the razor's edge. He likes risks and challenges. He likes confrontation and whoever puts up a fight.

One day, in England, he found one of those challengers: Graeme Souness, then coach of Blackburn. At Stamford Bridge the proximity of the benches gives rise to this kind of dispute, as Silvino Louro tells us: "The Scotsman wanted his full-back to go up on the pitch. Mourinho understood his intention and asked Robben not to accompany the Blackburn player: 'Stay! Stay!' But Souness provokingly decided to cut in the talk, saying to Robben 'Go! Go!' Minutes later we had the ball, a pass to Robben, who was alone, and goal to Chelsea. Souness turned to Mourinho and said: 'You've already screwed me!'"

It was one more of the 150 consecutive matches José Mourinho didn't lose at home. Nine years, divided by four clubs – FC Porto, Chelsea, Inter and Real Madrid – with 125 victories and 25 draws. A unique achievement in the history of football.

TENSE RELATIONSHIPS

His journey in the past decade has not always been a peaceful one. In over 500 games as head coach, Mourinho has fought terrible battles, not just with opponents, but with referees as well.

The first time he was sent off happened right in his debut season with FC Porto, against Benfica. In a tense match, as all the duels between these two teams are, Mourinho complained about a decision and referee João Ferreira sent him to the stand. At the end, Mourinho swore he hadn't said a word. The Dragons won 3-2. As coach for FC Porto he was expelled three more times, twice by the same referee: Pedro Proença. In each case Mourinho made a point of stressing he'd never offended the judges.

In England and Italy Mourinho's temper also earned him red cards. For example, when he was working for Inter, in the first year alone he suffered four expulsions.

The most curious episode happened on the Chelsea bench, when Mourinho actually expelled himself and the referee said no: "It was with one of the most qualified judges of the English League, Graham Poll. Zé wasn't happy with the refereeing. The ball went off across the touch line, by the bench, and he started yelling into the pitch, in the direction of the referee: 'You don't have the guts to blow the whistle! You're scared to blow the whistle!' As soon as he says this he jumps onto the stand, thinking he was going to be sent off. Funny enough, Poll called him and said: 'No, no, sit down on the bench, that's where I want you.' Even Mourinho himself was surprised", tells Rui Faria, who followed this episode from a metre away.

A HUMBLE, LOYAL OPPONENT

Looking back I miss the battles we fought in Portugal, he as coach for FC Porto, I sitting on the Benfica bench. Porto had a very strong team, perhaps the best in Europe at the time. They won everything. And Mourinho's brand was present in every aspect.

The Portugal Cup final arrived, in 2004. We were the ones who had to play against them. It was a really important game for us. Benfica was badly in need of a title and, what's more, against FC Porto. Fortunately we made it, in a very disputed, tremendously difficult game. It wasn't a victory of Camacho over Mourinho, but of Benfica against Porto. And he acknowledged defeat very well at the end. We hugged and he congratulated me.

There was a lot of rivalry between FC Porto and Benfica. In Lisbon the pressure to beat FC Porto, at any rate, was huge. But it wasn't easy. Their team was much better than Benfica's.

Despite this rivalry, we always knew how to keep things separate and built a deep affection for each other. He also knew how hard it was to coach Benfica, because he'd already done it. At that time, I was living a very sensitive situation. I felt the pressure to do something important in the club. I will always be grateful to him for having understood my problem and always expressed his solidarity. That also shows what a good person he is.

In FC Porto, Mourinho managed to build a solid group, with very progressive ideas about football for the time. It will be very difficult to have in Portugal another team that will supplant Mourinho's.

I was already familiar with José Mourinho's work from the time in Barcelona, and from his passage through União de Leiria and Benfica. When we met as opponents I was already aware that he was shaping himself to be the best coach in the world. That was obvious, due to the knowledge I had and to the way he drew a whole team behind him.

I saw him with a temper, with a lot of ambition and, above all, with a lot of knowledge. The most important thing in football is knowing you can learn with everyone and he had that capacity to learn. He absorbed everything like a sponge and now he is the one with the capacity to teach others.

A curious episode happened when I was in Benfica. At a certain point, we rehearsed a side free kick several times in training, by placing the ball at the entrance of the area for someone to show up and score. But in football, strategy moves are only good when they result in a goal.

Meanwhile, in an FC Porto match, they managed to score an important goal, resorting to the kind of move we'd rehearsed so often. At the end of the game, Mourinho had the humility to say that FC Porto had scored a goal with a "Camacho-style free kick". And that's how that move was called forever. I was thrilled, especially for José Mourinho's sincere personality.

He raises the figure of coach to the highest level possible, in the sense that in the teams, everyone knows he's the best. In that, Mourinho's the best, it's unquestionable. He defends his team, his players, his club, his fans till the end, there's no question about that.

Now Mourinho has hit the greatest challenge of his career. He's at a club where anything he does echoes enormously, whether in favour or against. That's Real Madrid for you. It's such a universal club, such a big club that any statement he makes has enormous reverberation. On the other hand, Mourinho himself is already so well known in the football world that he's always the talk of the town.

Mourinho did what he had to do in a club like that. He arrived and said: "I'm in charge here!" When you have this kind of personality and you can count on the president's unconditional support, you can take on the world. Then, you add to that good ideas and competence.

People must be patient and not pressure him, because results will show up. I believe this Real Madrid will end the Super Barcelona cycle, and that will be a remarkable feat.

JOSE ANTONIO CAMACHO

IN REAL MADRID...

"His degree of identification with the club surprised me! Mourinho opened our eyes about this thing of being a gentleman's club: they hurt us and we still congratulate them? It's not right and that has to be said, politely"

FLORENTINO PÉREZ

"Real Madrid needed a coach like Mourinho to recover values that were being lost"

HUGO SÁNCHEZ

R eal Madrid is the top of all clubs", said José Mourinho on 20th of September 2010, the day before he celebrated one decade as head coach. This phrase needs a context. The coach was referring to the club's history, magnitude and huge global impact, with the eyes of someone who had just arrived and was observing the phenomenon from the outside.

But Mourinho's mission as coach of Real Madrid required a different 'lens'. Once he made it to the top of the club – "to the Moon", as he himself once said – José Mourinho wasn't going to hang around dumbfounded and goggle-eyed, contemplating the work of art and the conquered trophies, submitting to the powers that be and to the amazing political wheeling and dealing. Because it's huge, because it's the "top of all clubs", Real Madrid is also the most coveted. There are plenty of people out there who dream of coaching it, want to run it or plan to preside over it.

Unlike the vast majority of coaches who passed through the casa blanca, Mourinho wasn't about to stand by doing nothing and watch the daily, deaf, often cynical contamination of his work. Mourinho likes to impose his rhythm and his method on the circumstances, tuning the whole club to the same wavelength. It was never in him to adapt to the circumstances, especially when these are unfavourable to him.

In other words, José Mourinho, coach of Real Madrid, would be no different from the one who triumphed in FC Porto, Chelsea or Inter. Without his traditional suit – or legendary overcoat -, and using a more sporty style (due to the new sponsor), the Portuguese coach would maintain the coherence that always characterised him. The only difference would be the club.

The first weeks were used to understand the inner workings. One of the areas needing intervention was the adversaries' scouting department. As in Inter, Mourinho took one of the men he trusted, José Morais, to coordinate this area. But otherwise both the collaborators and the way of producing information underwent substantial changes.

Six people were now working tirelessly on the production of reports, under the supervision of one of José Morais' men. The dynamic, the quality and the precision were changed. The adversaries' scouting department refined its work even more than it had done in Inter Milan.

Two scouts went all over Spain and the world, following the opponents. Each rival deserved at least four match observations in loco and perhaps two more games on video, to confirm details regarding dead balls and the like. The collection of information was carried out two weeks before the game at stake. Eight to ten days before, the survey was complete. With the time left, the opponent continued under watch to identify other details: which 'eleven' were going to play, if there were alterations imposed by injuries or punishments, and so on.

All the information was processed with software such as Amisco or MediaCoach. These are tools that provide all the data on the players' statistical behaviour: runs through centre, shots on the goal, assists, goals, rate of success, strongest foot, to which side they dribble and how... Well, absolutely everything. It's as important to identify the problems as it is to provide the solutions.

The work of the scouting department was supplemented by the art of the staff in charge of processing the information in an attractive way, to then be presented to the players. Two image editors made videos where the most important moves were highlighted. At the same time, two graphic designers prepared an illustrated folder (a kind of small newspaper) with photos taken from the videos, focusing on details that were important to underline. These were the two forms of help Mourinho presented to the players before the games. But there was more. With the information available, the Portuguese coach would gradually introduce in the training sessions certain situations that he wished to apply in the match at stake, long before it took place. It was a subtle way of working on the players' subconscious and 'put them in the game.'

The urgency of the calendar, with matches every three days, complicated the life of the department. Sometimes, by coincidence, three or four opponents would be simultaneously under observation. 'Organisation' was the motto.

Despite the huge internal and external difficulties, José Mourinho achieved important sporting results right in the first season. In just one year, the Merengues recovered the Spanish Cup (absent from the Bernabéu for 18 years), reached the Champions League semi-finals (a competition in which Real Madrid hadn't even got to the eighth-finals in the previous six years, even losing its seeded status) and they still put at attention FC Barcelona, which had hitherto been ruling unchallenged.

It would have been almost impossible to do better in what was, to all intents and purposes, his 'year zero'. While he shaped the team to his image every day, so as to break down the Catalan wall, he still had to spend his energy on the internal reconstitution of the Club, fighting against unexpected obstacles. It was like moving mountains. In January 2011, just six months after he'd entered the Club, in an interview for the newspaper O Jogo, Mourinho was already putting his finger on the problem: "Real Madrid is a difficult challenge because, in my opinion as observer – despite living within the club for half a dozen months, I'm still an observer -, it's a club that isn't structured for its magnitude".

Due to all this, the 2010/11 season was completely exhausting. So much so that, in February 2011, he announced on Real Madrid TV that he'd gone to downtown Madrid only two or three times: "I don't know Madrid. I go from my house to Valdebebas every day and little else. I've been to downtown Madrid two or three times since I got here." Concentration at work was, and is, absolute. As Mourinho said in the same interview, "there are a lot of people who get into the big clubs as a career objective. The objective isn't to get here, it's to win. I often say to my players that getting to a big club only means something if you win something in the end, if you say 'I played in Real, Milan or Manchester and I won a lowly cup', it means nothing." Several "lowly cups" were awaiting José Mourinho in Real Madrid.

THE FIRST CRATERS

In November 2010, five months after having taken control of the Merengue club, José Mourinho wrote the preface of the book "Bible of Real Madrid" (published by Prime Books), with the following passage: "I am on the moon, but with my feet firmly on the ground. I wish to praise the culture and tradition of Real Madrid, based on a dominant football. This is the club's DNA, we cannot and should not forget it." Mourinho would honour the Madridista values and tradition, but… But he'd already realised that that moon wasn't perfect. It had craters, most of them hidden. Genuine traps!

Over time, José Mourinho discovered the lunar side of this planet called Real Madrid.

The internal game of interests prevented the Portuguese coach from putting into practice one of his most important recipes for success: unity. Valdano was the most visible face of the blockade, the core of a dominant trend for years and years.

The first warning to the then general manager came during a press conference, after a match in which the referee did a really bad job. Mourinho was given by the Club structure a paper with the referee's list of mistakes. But instead of reading the list out, he preferred to show the paper and explain to the journalists how ridiculous it was to hand over to the coach the task of reporting refereeing mistakes. With a simple wave of a sheet of paper, Mourinho bared Real Madrid and showed the world its frailties.

The shockwaves with Valdano grew. This conflict had a history behind it. When José Mourinho was still running Chelsea, between 2005 and 2008, Valdano was busy throwing darts at him through articles he wrote: "Problematic" or "a wandering charisma that doesn't know what it represents", were some of the considerations he used to qualify Mourinho. On the day of his presentation, on 31ˢᵗ May 2010, Valdano attempted to calm the waters by assuring that his quarrel with Mourinho had been "solved three years ago". But time proved him wrong. And the war continued in Madrid, with fiery episodes:

19th September 2010 – Prevented from coaching Portugal

Carlos Queiroz is sacked from his position as national coach. The Portuguese federation tries to hire Mourinho part-time, combining this with the position of Real Madrid coach. Mourinho wants to, but Valdano doesn't let him.

16th October 2010 – Prince of Asturias

José Mourinho guaranteed that no Real Madrid player would attend the ceremony for the Prince of Asturias award to the Spanish team. The following day Valdano contradicts him: "Iker Casillas will go."

29th November 2010 –Higuaín's injury

The Argentine forward is diagnosed with a slipped disc. Mourinho advocates his immediate surgery, the club doesn't. Mourinho feels his authority is undermined.

30th November 2010 – Hugo Almeida denied

Mourinho wants to reinforce his attack during the winter market. The 'nine' he chooses is Hugo Almeida. Valdano denies his wish and tries Van Nistelrooy. The coach talks about "cats and dogs."

19th December 2010 – Refereeing mistakes

The famous sheet of paper with the 13 refereeing mistakes made during the Real Madrid – Seville match was a pretext for Mourinho to accuse Valdano of not defending the club. The leader replied that Real never talks about referees.

16th January 2011 – A 'nine' on the bench

The tug-of-war for a striker goes on. Drawing 1-1 in Almería revives the debate. Valdano says: "I see a 'nine' on the bench (Benzema)." The following day, Mourinho lets it be known that he wants to leave.

24th January 2011 – Imminent breach

Despite a series of denials by Valdano, dealing with the Portuguese coach is unbearable. Mourinho is asked about the hiring of a forward. He replies: "I only report to Florentino and José Ángel". The next day, Adebayor arrives.

25th January 2011 – Forbidden to travel with the team

Valdano was part of the committee that, the day before the games away, travelled with the team. Up to Seville – Real Madrid. That day, Mourinho forbade him to come on board, and from that day onwards the general manager began to travel with Florentino Pérez.

26th January 2011 – Forbidden to contact the players

in Valdebebas, Mourinho puts an end to Jorge Valdano's contacts with the players in the Sports City of Valdebebas.

1st February 2011 – Contract renewals

Mourinho doesn't understand why the club accelerates Sérgio Ramos' renewal but keeps stalling the extension of Pepe's. The fact that this Luso-Brazilian is represented by Jorge Mendes is not strange to the coach's doubt.

10th May 2011 – Silencing criticism

The sequence of criticism regarding refereeing and stated by José Mourinho comes to a truce after the game between Real Madrid and Getafe. Valdano uses the occasion to goad him: "He'd better take one step back." The coach's spokesman, Eládio Paramés, answers: "Mourinho will talk and make noise whenever he feels it is appropriate."

The split happened, at long last, at the end of the 2010/11 season. On 26th May 2011, Florentino Pérez summoned a press conference to present Real Madrid's new organisation chart. The president's sentence that made headlines was to be: "Real Madrid's sports spokesman will be Mourinho."

The Portuguese coach thus won an unthinkable tug-of-war and took on the full powers of the club. He wasn't just the sports spokesman – as Florentino had said –, he was the new manager of the club, an unprecedented position in the centennial history of Real Madrid.

The exit of the general manager, by itself, wouldn't wipe away all the sand off the mechanism. Time had left many vices and traces. The issue wasn't going be solved with band-aids. A deep surgery was needed. That's why Mourinho asked Florentino Pérez for some autonomy in the sports management. In other words, full powers in his field.

The Club's new organisation chart was to have one less step: the position of general sports manager, previously occupied by Jorge Valdano. That position would be taken over by José Ángel Sánchez. In other words, José Mourinho would depend directly on Ángel Sánchez. He would report to him, and only to him. The challenge was 'simple': to change Real Madrid – from head to toe, sweeping every single area of the giant.

A NEW ORDER

The new Merengue order emerged at the start of the 2011/12 season. With the 'moon' clear of craters (at least the largest and most dangerous ones), José Mourinho found that extra motivation to embark on the 'all or nothing' season.

The details that usually make the difference started stirring up in Mourinho's mind. The first sign showed in the pre-season kickoff, scheduled for a Monday, 11th July. But the Portuguese coach issued a collective order; he wanted everyone to be there, at their respective homes in Madrid, one day earlier, on 10th July. This way there would be no last-minute delays, as is often the case with players coming from other continents.

The team travelled to the United States, where it opened the season's preparation with three private games. Before leaving, there was a previous meeting in Valdebebas for the required medical tests. José Mourinho was the first to arrive, punctually, at 7.40 in the morning. Before any other member of the technical team, or any player or leader, he was opening the doors of the Sports City and setting the example.

There was a surprise in the committee that travelled to Los Angeles: Paul Burguess, Real Madrid's English groundsman. The specialist in grass fields, hired from Arsenal, came along at Mourinho's express request. He wanted Burguess to prepare the grass of the North Athletic Fields (the pre-season training centre) to the liking of the players and of the technical team.

Another of José Mourinho's claims became public at the season's start: Alex, a cook, was hired. The new recruit also came to the United States where, alongside Jesús González (better known as Chechu), then the Club's chef, he was in charge of gradually introducing certain novelties in the athletes' diet.

Hiring the new cook brought along new habits to Valdebebas. During the first months of the season, eating in the sports city became compulsory, with menus supervised by a sports-specialised nutritionist. In the past, Bernd Schuster had already introduced this habit of eating at Valdebebas, when he coached Real Madrid, but not in a mandatory way, only to promote the group spirit. At the start of the 2011/12 season, everything changed. In a small, cosy room not far from the changing room, three rows of tables and some sofas were set up. At one end of the room, the buffet with salads, pastas, fish and meat. The layout of the space was strategically inviting for social interaction. A TV set was always on in one of the corners. But it wasn't on a Spanish or international channel, nor did it show films or series. The TV in the Valdebebas dining room showed videos, graphically worked on by the scouting department, with moves of the next Merengue opponent. The players were digesting their food and, at the same time, their opponents' characteristics.

We must add that Chechu, the Valdebebas chef during Mourinho's first season, ended up leaving Real Madrid in the summer of 2011, four years after entering the Club. He definitely didn't have the profile Mourinho wanted. And perhaps this statement by Chechu, in an interview for El País when he entered Real Madrid, may help explain the Portuguese coach's decision – "I'm not a fanatic. I'm not a Madrid supporter, but I'm not anti-Madrid either."

Mourinho's 'tentacles' literally touched every area: from the medical department to security, from marketing to communications. The changes in the clinical area shocked the Club and offended many internal sensibilities. Hernández Yáñez, who had been the Merengue doctor for over a decade, left the group. The Portuguese coach also asked for a physical trainer-therapist and the subsequent redundancies of several professionals who worked in Valdebebas, as a result of the protocol between Madrid and the Sanitas clinic for football and basketball. Mourinho couldn't imagine Real Madrid without their own health professionals, paid by the Club and subject to the same discipline. One year's experience in 2010/11 with an external clinical team had been enough for Mourinho to detect serious flaws, namely regarding inside information leaks.

The so-called 'information filter feeders' kept coming out from under the stones. Mourinho went to the point of saying that Real Madrid was a club where "the walls talk and have ears". Everyone had a friend in the press, from the managers to the kit staff. Naturally Óscar Ribot, Press Chief for Real Madrid, also left the Club at the 2012/13 season kickoff. He'd occupied the position for three years, but never resisted promoting relations with the players, more than was advisable for someone in charge of the press. The former As journalist, who had entered the Club in 2009 through Florentino Pérez, was replaced by Carlos Carbajosa, a journalist coming directly from the El Mundo newsroom.

With or without Óscar Ribot, the truth is that with José Mourinho, communications in Real Madrid underwent a radical change in its philosophy. "Now the press knows things when we want them to know and not as it was before", he warned during the 2011/12 pre-season, clearly referring to what happened when Jorge Valdano was general director of sports.

The North-American pre-season training programme in Los Angeles set the new order: in 13 days, not one player turned up in the press room; Mourinho didn't give a single interview; and all the elements of the staff had specific orders not to talk, even if informally, with the journalists. Another phenomenon was the average age of the players who came to California – 24.8 years of age. In that season (2011/12), the Real Madrid team was the eighth youngest in the world. New contracts with Varane (18), Sahin (22), Coentrão (23) and Callejón (24) literally brought new blood into the team. Mourinho's 'new order' was regarding the Club in terms of its future.

José Mourinho gave daily lessons on competence, planning and rigour. That was the main obstacle in the way of his critics: they had nothing to go on to question his professionalism. Four months after the 2010/11 season began, an illustrative episode happened. Something new came up on Real Madrid's competitive calendar. For the first time, the team would be playing at midday (for the League against Osasuna) because of commitments with the Chinese market. Mourinho surprised again in the little things. Realising his players were too used to the night shift (being the team that had had most matches at 10 pm), he decided to change the athletes' biological clock. The week before the duel, he marked all the training sessions for the time of the game. And on the Friday, 48 hours before the match, he imposed a daily routine identical to that of the day of the match: breakfast, rest, lecture and warm-up for the game. Two days later Real Madrid thrashed Osasuna, 7-1.

HIRING RIGOUR

When he assumed the command of Real Madrid, José Mourinho inherited a set of questionable contracts, to say the least. Players such as Pedro León, Sergio Canales and Esteban Granero, all the responsibility of the sports director Jorge Valdano, weren't at all missed at the Bernabéu, having been the source of tension during Mourinho's first season (2010/11).

The case of Pedro León was well known. This player came from Múrcia to Madrid as a rising star of the Spanish football panorama. One good season with Getafe was enough to earn the huge responsibility of wearing the white shirt in exchange for a mighty 10 million Euros. Mourinho needed only a few weeks to come to the opposite conclusion. Pedro León used to train without intensity and almost always badly – two problems that, in Mourinho's book, usually mean 'goodbye'. And so it did. León left the frontline of sports options, but stayed in the limelight of the political options. Don't forget that he was one of Jorge Valdano's bets. And the press did its job, asking Mourinho why he wasn't using the player. Towards the end of September 2010, on the eve of a Champions game against Auxerre, the topic returned to the press room: "Why did you leave Pedro León out of the squad?" Mourinho decided, there and then, to make things very clear: "You talk about Pedro León as if he were Maradona or Zidane. He'll play when he works the way I want and it'll be more difficult for him to play when he doesn't". And that was that. At the end of the season León went back to Getafe, on loan. Three months after leaving Real Madrid, Pedro León bled all his hatred for José Mourinho, even accusing him of having blocked his departure to Chelsea in the winter market. Time has shown that, under Mourinho's command or elsewhere, León never deserved all that attention and so he stayed with Getafe. During that same meeting with the press, the player would eventually show his true colours with this phrase: "I found great people at Real Madrid, like Valdano, Pardeza, and Butrageño. They're first-class, especially Jorge Valdano who is a true gentleman". There you go.

The new order imposed by Mourinho from the 2011/12 season onwards also impacted the hiring area: tight standards and confidentiality. Mourinho set up a very restricted elite group, to make decisions. Calejón was an emblematic example: for two months, negotiations were deadlocked between Florentino Pérez, José Angel Sánchez, Zidane (then sports director) and Mourinho himself.

The coach's direct intervention in hiring also proved valuable. For example, Nuri Sahin confessed he felt flattered with Mourinho's phone call: "I pick up the phone, I say 'hello?' and I hear 'hi, this is Mourinho'. I thought someone was pulling my leg! He told me he'd followed me throughout the whole season with Dortmund and he wanted me on the team". At the closure of 2011, Souleymane Coulibaly – the 17-year-old Ivory Coast player considered the 'new Drogba' – also explained what he felt when he heard Real Madrid was interested in him: "Being the object of Mourinho's interest is like going to Disneyland when you're a kid, it's like living in a dream land".

REINTERPRETATION OF THE TERM SEÑORÍO

For many years, decades even, Real Madrid had no need of politics or of reinforcing its ideology. They kept winning and that was it. The club and the fans rested by their trophies and fell asleep in the comfort of their glories. They developed a sort of second skin that could make them immune and superior in relation to the other clubs. The term señorío took roots during this period. Convinced of their untouchability, Real Madrid gradually lost track of reality in the same proportion as they lost their domain in the world of sports.

FC Barcelona was able to understand its own weaknesses and got a move on. During the period prior to the Dream Team, right in the middle of the Merengue golden era, they built an ideological concept based on political ideals and on an artificial victimization strategy. Certain Barcelona intellectuals, such as writer Manuel Vásquez Montalbán, actively participated in this process. It was in this ideological setting that Xavi, Iniesta, Valdés, Busquets, Messi, Piqué, and Puyol grew, and Montoya, Tello, Deulofeu and many others continue to grow. Besides an excellent football school, La Masia also created and developed an ideology. It's something you don't see, but that is present in Xavi's leadership, or in Puyol's character, as well as in Alves' simulations or in Busquets' exhibitions.

Comfortably sitting on their untouchable condition of señorío, Real Madrid allowed themselves to be overtaken. When they woke up, Barça had already built the Dream Team and the Pep Team, won Leagues and Champions, and was ruling over Spanish and world football. FC Barcelona became a respected, winning team that was praised all over the world. Everything that had once belonged to Real Madrid.

This is the point in time when José Mourinho walks in. The Portuguese coach landed at the Bernabéu, on 31st May 2010, precisely to dynamite the Azulgrana supremacy and return those credentials lost by Real Madrid. Reversing in a couple of years the course of a history built over a decade was a herculean task. Mourinho took it up, with some firm ideas from the start. One of them was that they were in no situation to keep up the condition of señorío as untouchable. This would be an all-out war.

One by one, Mourinho opened the trapdoors strategically placed in the way of Real Madrid. Bluntly, he criticised referee performances, timeframes, journalists, opponents, coaches, FIFA, UEFA and even the inside enemies who crossed his path, like Valdano and Toril.

It was an extremely risky, rapid-wear strategy for Mourinho's image. Practically on his own, he took ownership of all the consequences, both internal and external. He collected fines and sanctions. The heaviest one of his career happened in November 2010, when the UEFA decreed five games' suspension – four effective ones and the fifth with a three-year suspended sentence – and a 50,000 euro fine, for misconduct during the Champions League. The most important European football institution considered "inappropriate" José Mourinho's statements after beating Barcelona in the semi-finals (0-2), when Pepe was sent off: "I don't know if it's because of UNICEF, I don't know if it's José María Villar's power (president of the Spanish Football Federation and of the UEFA Arbitration Board). I don't understand. If I say what I think, my career ends here", vented Mourinho. In July 2011, the UEFA Appeals Committee decided to ease the punishment applied: the same five games' suspension, but only three effective ones and two with a three-year suspended sentence. The 50,000 euro fine was upheld.

Mourinho's behaviour was fiercely attacked by the more conservative Madridista sectors and by certain fake self-righteous blanca puritans who cynically hitched a ride.

It remained to be seen whether this path chosen by the Portuguese coach really hurt the values of Madridism. It was important to understand if the members – the true representatives of the Club – disapproved of the anti-señorío method. The answer arrived on 26th September 2011, during the General Meeting of Committed Members. When Florentino Pérez's intervention emphasised José Mourinho's name for the first time, the auditorium of the Conference and Exhibition Centre interrupted his speech with a 42-second ovation. That day, the president of Real Madrid let it be clearly known that the Club had entered another 'Era'. He also guaranteed that the face of this change would be José Mourinho: "I too am surprised with Mourinho's degree of identification with the club. He opened our eyes about this señorío thing. Señorío is reporting when a player throws himself on the ground and fakes. Mourinho has the support of 95% of the members". Maybe Florentino wasn't far from the real percentage. Never had a Real Madrid coach made such a deep impression, in such little time. After a few months in Madrid, the Bernabéu already had a song devoted to him, chanted game after game.

Some of the Club's notables, true Madridistas, went even further in defending the strategy used by Mourinho. Hugo Sánchez, for instance, actually declared that "Real Madrid needed a coach like Mourinho to recover values that were being lost".

"About this thing of being a gentleman's club… They hurt us and we still congratulate them? It's not right and that has to be said, politely", stated Florentino Pérez on more than one occasion. It was clear that, from then on, Real Madrid wouldn't turn the other cheek.

For everyone to understand better, José Mourinho preferred to explain on the field what this señorío business really is. On 18th September 2012, after Real Madrid performed an epic turnaround at the Bernabéu, against Manchester City – from 1-2 to 3-2 – the Portuguese coach gave practical examples of his interpretation of señorío: "Today this team showed it has Real Madrid DNA. This is the señorío. Señorío is dying on the pitch, as these players showed", he explained moments after having kneeled on the grass to celebrate the last-minute goal that got Real Madrid through to the Champions eighth-finals.

A month later, in an interview for Real Madrid TV, Mourinho explained the concept a little better: "I'm nothing, or very little, in the history of Real Madrid. I only won the Liga 32, a Cup we hadn't won in many years, and a Supercup, very little for Real Madrid's history. I only spoke about the señorío because there's a misconception because of many people, who are no longer in the club, and who sold a wrong idea of señorío. A Real Madrid player has to die, so to speak, on the pitch. Real Madrid players have to reach the end of the match exhausted".

EVERYTHING BUT A SAINT

They've called him Jew, torturer, con man, evil, Nazi, pathetic, manipulative; they compare him to monkeys or to absolutist dictators; they say he warps history or that he's a harmful character for Real Madrid; and on the day Bin Laden was killed, someone was even capable of drawing a parallel between the terrorist's death and the Portuguese coach's layoff. For three years, José Mourinho heard and read the most atrocious things about himself, in the Spanish media.

Mourinho faced new codes, very different from the ones he'd found in the other countries where he'd worked. In Portugal, extreme 'clubitis' stifled some opinions and Mourinho's hubris gathered no sympathy either, but there was always loyalty in the analyses made and the titles eventually gifted the relationship with respect. In England, the Portuguese coach was always admired by the media. And in Italy, Mourinho knew what he could (or could not) count on from the start. At least in Milan: the media were almost totally dominated by the owner of the main rival (Sílvio Berlusconi), Milan, so it was mandatory to deal with this fait accompli.

In Spain the scenario was much more incoherent. Swampy, even. The strength of the Spanish sports press, coupled with its tremendous capacity of influence over the protagonists, was unlikely to be compatible with José Mourinho's strong personality. On top of all this there was a 'world apart', called Real Madrid. A club loaded with internal and external interests, capable of directly influencing the life of the institution. Raw sports politics, every single day. To make it even worse, Mourinho probably found the European country with most hours of information dedicated to sports. Spanish sports journalism desperately needs protagonists, news, debates, speculation on a daily basis, and a lot of hours of material to feed various radio and TV shows, newspaper pages and the internet.

The Spanish journalists grew more and more impatient as José Mourinho compulsively refused the overwhelming majority of their requests for interviews. The fingers of one hand are enough to count the exclusives Mourinho gave the Spanish media in three years: only Marca, Cadena SER, As and ABC, besides his interviews for the Club's official television channel (Real Madrid TV). This was unthinkable for a press used to the protagonists' full availability! Instead, José Mourinho multiplied his exclusives for Portugal, England, Italy, and France, which the Spanish journalists were forced to quote, in order to have news. Mourinho also radically changed the team's contact with the media: journalists out of the team's plane and of the training centre, open sessions lasting only 15 minutes, only one player available to talk before the games and total silence from all the protagonists. José Ramón de la Morena, host of the show "El Larguero" of Cadena SER, was among the first to pass a sentence of retaliation against the new rules: "How can those in charge of informing write good things after this slap in the face?"

José Mourinho was caught in the line of fire and also in the cross-fire, acting as a human shield for the president. He took many lost bullets whose target was Florentino Pérez, especially from the moment the relationship between Mourinho and Valdano went sour and the sports director's exit became inevitable. The decision to dismiss Valdano, giving over to Mourinho full powers, only roused the detractors' desire for revenge. Masks fell. Mourinho bought himself a war – the greatest of all in his career – until the end of his days in Madrid.

EL PAIS OF INSULTS

In a profile called "José Mourinho, the hooligan coach", published on the 28th January 2012 in El País, the English journalist John Carlin wrote this: "The immaturity of a teenager and the intolerance of a military dictator shake his contradictory personality", and this: "It would be no exaggeration to say that he is a candidate for the most divisive character since the days of General Franco". Álvaro Faes, of the daily La Nueva España, called him "arrogant, right-wing, Catholic and whose family is linked to the dictator Salazar". During an ONA FM radio broadcast, one reporter let the following pearl slip out: "Yesterday Bin Laden fell, today Mourinho falls". In August 2011, while the El País film critic, Carlos Boyero, replied to readers' questions in a digital meeting, one user stated: "Mourinho is a very dangerous individual. And he knows how to get the worst out of people. Indeed, football can be a sport played mainly be men. Not by animals." Boyero answered with the following commentary: "That's what the Portuguese Nazi wants". This phrase was also rewarded with legal proceedings on behalf of Mourinho's lawyers.

In fact, El País became a genuine case study in the matter of persecution, while Mourinho headed Real Madrid. Such a violent attack of the Prisa newspaper on a Merengue coach is quite unprecedented. Equally unparalleled is an aggressive column written by José Sámano, head of the sports section of El País, on 19th September 2012, called "Mou's column". Two days earlier, Real Madrid had beaten Manchester City (3-2) at the Bernabéu, at the opening match of the Champions League group stage. Sámano ignored all the virtues of winning and preferred to discuss the alleged censorship that Mourinho imposes on journalists and even on his players: "The Real Madrid coach denies journalists precisely what he denies his players: freedom of expression". Further on, he concludes: "To Mou, the press is just a loudspeaker at his beck and call. In a way he's right, because there are lots of people like him who only see journalists as their bag carriers: me, me and me; or against god (he'd put the divine capital letter)".

Whoever read the Spanish press would think that coaching Real Madrid was a minor detail in the life of José Mourinho. He was under fire every day. Sometimes it would come from where it was least expected. Even the retired José María García went 'active' again, in a November 2012 edition of Marca's tuitcam, to praise Guardiola and classify José Mourinho and Florentino Pérez as an "evil duo" that "is forever damaging the history of Real Madrid".

After all, the true motive of such rage and the real reason for insults such as those we have read above, was a personal matter. Alfredo Di Stéfano, the Merengue myth and an undisputed defender of the Madridista values, summed it all up in a phrase he said during a radio sports program of the state-run Argentine news agency Télam: "The press doesn't like Mourinho because he's not nice. The journalists want him fired but the leaders and the fans defend him".

Except for the two legal proceedings against journalists José Sámano and Carlos Boyero, José Mourinho reacted icily to all the slander he suffered over three years. Unflinching, he didn't alter the planned route a single inch. This task is all the more difficult when you're managing the greatest giant of world football. Without batting an eyelid, Mourinho kept on going in the crossfire: "I'm not a child anymore, neither are my kids, and my wife is suffering with the disrespectful comments made about me, most of them for strategic reasons. But that doesn't tire me, it only saddens me. While my family is all right and I'm happy in Real Madrid, there'll be no problem", stated the Portuguese coach to the Club's channel in October 2012.

BETTER THAN 'THE BEST IN HISTORY'

"Look at them: The opponent puts out the red carpet for them, in a minute the referee's asking for an autograph… Rival fans go to the stadium just to see Barça. Tomorrow the papers, including Madrid's, are going to write about how great they are. If I go to the Bernabéu, I'll have to put a bomb on all this!" This was said by José Mourinho to his closest collaborators, after having watched a match with FC Barcelona, when he was still wearing Inter's colours.

As always, José Mourinho took the 'Real' challenge very seriously. His effort, dedication and greed for titles are in his DNA. However, this time it would be different. There was a Barça, considered unbeatable. There was the best coach in the world against the best team in the world. And to beat an exceptional Barça, it took exceptional measures. Mourinho knew that, even before arriving.

The merry-go-round began. The opening season confirmed his suspicions: that Barcelona was the strongest ever. A model sustained by layers and layers of years; the coincidence in time of a vast set of quality players; and the comfort of being able to work backed by the press (always kneeling at the club's feet) and a power system (clearly a friend in influencing internal and external decisions). On the other hand, 600 kilometres away, José Mourinho was about to discover the rocky path ahead: a highly politicised club; dangerous and comfortably established interests, capable of putting at risk the organisation of key areas; doors wide open to the press and to journalists running errands for various factions; contracts of a highly questionable value, as time would show.

The gargantuan nature of Real Madrid was directly proportional to the problems it dragged on. Its distance from Barça was much greater than those 600 kilometres. Mourinho could only rely on his trusted men and work full speed to fight this unequal battle. In time, he might count on the trust of a president who knew everything about management, but next to zero when it came to football. Mourinho would have to arduously pave the way for the future of Real Madrid. As clear as day.

THE FIRST WIN

Inspired by FC Barcelona, José Mourinho embarked on an internal revolution in Real Madrid. As we mentioned above, the manner of preparing the matches, for instance, changed radically in relation to what the Merengues used to do. And the conquest of the Copa del Rey in the opening season (2010/11) – Mourinho's first blanco title which Real Madrid had let slip for 18 years – was precisely based on the method of analysis of the opponent. Some days before the game, Mourinho gathered his collaborators and asked them for their opinion regarding the way the team should play. The four elements of the technical team came up with piles of solutions, all of them different, all of them fantastic. The chief heard them carefully and finally he concluded with a smile: "You're just complicating things, I'm more confused than I was before", turned his back and walked out of the room.

A few days later he called José Morais, who was in charge of the scouting department, and explained the strategy he had in mind, with a scheme and a game plan. He asked his collaborator for information that might supplement these ideas and their transposition to video and graphic means. Much of the work in that final had to do with the coach's ideas. He was the one to devise a plan to annul certain aspects of Barcelona's attacking game, while at the same time benefitting from a number of defensive frailties of the opponent, namely regarding the challenge of overcoming the first pressure line. Mourinho outlined, to perfection, the best way to halt FC Barcelona's strongest point: game organisation and the creation of attacking situations in the other half of the pitch, with Messi, Xavi and Iniesta, backed up by Dani Alves and by the constant disruptions by Pedro and Villa. The signature of Culer football – based on short moves, for 10 or 15 seconds, with a strong probability of a through-ball at any moment – was reduced to a minimum.

An important detail about winning the Copa del Rey was losing at Camp Nou for the championship, in that same season (2010/11). The biggest defeat in José Mourinho's career (5-0) served for him to clearly identify everything that should not be done. Right after the referee's final whistle, the Portuguese coach addressed the players with words of great confidence and hope in the future. Mourinho's resilient character emerged. That rare art of turning weakness into strength. Strange as it may seem, this crushing defeat became one of the most positive moments of the season.

The duels Ronaldo/Messi, Mourinho/Guardiola, and Real Madrid/ FC Barcelona marked the 2010/11 season. There were four scorching, high strung derby matches, played in just 19 days. The first, for the League, ended in a 1-1 draw. Far from glorifying the beauty of football, this match allowed José Mourinho to make a stand and bare his teeth at the rival. The coach's surprise move was to place Pepe in the centre midfield.

The Copa del Rey final came next, and Mourinho had more tricks up his sleeve. Pepe stayed in the centre and the team played higher up on the field. Cristiano Ronaldo scored the winning goal, in extra time. One more detail: Iker Casillas. He covered all the holes in the goal mouth during the most difficult part of the game. Here, too, Mourinho's psychological work was decisive. He knew how to explore the importance of this title for the goalkeeper, and to the benefit of the whole team. The Copa del Rey was the trophy missing in Casillas' long list of triumphs. Therefore, Mourinho put him in the starting lineup during the whole campaign (750 minutes) and got decisive performances in return. Casillas ran after his dream throughout the whole season: to lift the Copa del Rey. And he managed to, with a fantastic match against FC Barcelona. At the end of the Copa del Rey, it was proved Barça could be broken on the pitch.

Whoever was stunned with this win, in Mourinho's opening year, must know nothing of his past. He is a true specialist in national cups. And FC Barcelona should have known that. In his 10 years of activity, Mourinho was a finalist or semi-finalist in seven of them, with four trophies to show his grandchildren, one from each country where he coached: Portugal (FC Porto – 2002/03); England (Chelsea – 2006/07); Italy (Inter – 2009/10); and Spain (Real Madrid – 2010/11).

With respect to derbies, in his first season in Madrid, the Champions semi-final draw result put the icing on his cake, with a match between Real Madrid and FC Barcelona. It wasn't yet the ideal moment for the Merengue team, and Mourinho knew it. But the match had to be played. Despite everything, the recent past brought a speck of hope. The first leg at the Bernabéu was balanced, as the result showed (0-0), until Pepe was sent off. This fact was to decide the qualifying round because, with such an imbalance of forces, Messi scored twice and everything was practically decided there and then. Mourinho realised that, protested a lot and also got sent off. The game at Camp Nou ended in a 1-1 tie (Pedro and Marcelo) and further controversy: Higuaín had his goal annulled. Casillas and Xabi Alonso talked about stealing.

With the exception of the first match for the League, which was quite atypical (5-0), the 2010/11 battle with Barça came to one win, one loss and two ties. Not bad for year one, particularly if we consider something Mourinho has repeated several times: "My second years are the best."

The real truth is that the Azulgrana empire only came down with the direct intervention of the Portuguese coach. Guardiola's Super-Barça only lost three titles out of 13: one Champions League and two Copas del Rey. In two of these – Champions and one Copa del Rey – Mourinho was sitting on the opponent's bench. Throughout his career, he went up against Pep Guardiola on nine occasions. He lost only four times.

THE END OF THE CATALAN SUPREMACY

It was his awareness of details that allowed José Mourinho to over-throw what many considered to be the "best team in the world", or, better yet, the "best team in history": FC Barcelona, Spanish champion for three consecutive years (2008/09, 2009/10 and 2010/11) before the Portuguese coach arrived.

Mourinho listened to these labels for many months. He heard them and endured them, in silence. When Real Madrid won the 2011/12 League, he broke loose and said everything that had been choking him: "We won against one of the best teams in history, but some enlightened beings think the football they play is the only one that exists", he started by saying. "Those people only know about football through Google. They click on their computer and absorb knowledge. But football is more than that. We played in a spectacular way, we scored a bunch of goals and we got a lot of wins", concluded Mourinho.

The only coach who was champion in three of the main European Leagues – England, Italy and Spain – was absolutely right. If that Barça was one of the best teams in history, where did that put the club that had just robbed it of its title?

As José Mourinho stated, Real Madrid had an astounding season. It had won the best Spanish League in history, with some crazy records. Among many landmarks, it beat the mythic record of scored goals (121), which belonged to Toshack's Real Madrid (107); it beat the record of wins (32 out of 38); it got the best goal difference (between scored and conceded goals), 89; Cristiano Ronaldo scored 46 goals, Benzema over 30; it certified its title at Camp Nou, home to the supposedly "best team in history"; and, above all, it scored 100 points, something no other team had ever achieved before, beating the 99-point record that belonged to Pep Guardiola's 2009/10 Barcelona ... the famous "best in history".

In recent times it wouldn't have been possible to find a season where Real Madrid had won more titles than Barcelona. It had happened a decade before, in 2001/02, when the Madridistas won the Champions, the League, the European Supercup and the Intercontinental Cup. In 2011/12, against the "best Barça in history", Madrid overtook its rival again: the Catalans got the Copa del Rey and Messi's 90 goals; the Merengues took the League, the Spain Supercup (also conquered from Barça) and had a superb season played by Cristiano Ronaldo, though not enough to win the Golden Ball. The team did the best first round of all time in the League; also in the League, it turned losing results around in 9 games; it made 25 consecutive wins in matches for the League and for Champions; and it continuously scored in 41 matches.

A highly symbolic sign of Merengue power was evident in the 2011/12 championship, against the two European League finalists in that year: Athletic Bilbau (4-1 and 3-0), and Atlético de Madrid (4-1 and 4-1), four thrashings!

Something that will also stay forever, as a brand image for the Merengue win, is Cristiano Ronaldo's gesture after defining the League at Camp Nou. The Portuguese player turned to the stand and said: "Don't worry, I'm here". During that season, he became the best Madridista scorer in a League, with 46 goals; he scored against all the teams in the championship, which had only happened once with César, in 1950/51; and he still did six hat-tricks, beating Lángara's and Romário's records (five).

José Mourinho got the best from his players. This is typical of him, but in 2011/12 he took it to the limit. Sports-wise, the players gave their all. Therefore, when he was called to the stage on the day of the championship celebration at the Santiago Bernabéu, Mourinho knelt on the grass in front of his troops. To the microphones he said: "You will always be the players of the 100-point League."

When Real Madrid won the League mathematically, against Athletic (3-0), the journalists asked the Portuguese coach how he was feeling. Mourinho replied: "I celebrated for five minutes and full stop. I want to see if tomorrow I can be with José Ángel to decide things and go to work." José Ángel Sánchez is the general director of Real Madrid, the man with whom José Mourinho decided the club's day to day (contracts, exemptions and other operational options). Some people thought Mourinho was exaggerating. Well. The team arrived in Madrid at 3 am, Mourinho said goodbye to the players, and the next morning he was at José Ángel's office to plan the 2012/13 season.

17 TIMES A DERBY

Sitting on the Real Madrid bench, José Mourinho fought 17 derbies against FC Barcelona in just three seasons. Barbaric! It means an average of over five matches per season against the same team, as emotionally charged as all derbies are.

Along the way, the Portuguese coach met three different coaches on the opposite side – Pep Guardiola, Tito Vilanova and Jordi Roura -, while the adversary always had the same opponent. It's true that the Azulgrana matrix is common to all three coaches, without major fluctuations in the game model. But it's also true that the psychological strain of 17 derbies was divided by three and the possibility to innovate was multiplied by the same number.

Reversing the cycle was a matter of time. An overwhelmingly victorious cycle of Barcelona over Real Madrid. It's good to remind those who are more absent-minded that in the two seasons prior to José Mourinho's arrival – 2008/09 and 2009/10 – Madrid and Barça encountered one another only four times, always for the championship, with 100% negative results for the Merengues: four defeats. And in the midst of this dark scenario is one of the biggest humiliations inflicted by the Catalans at the Bernabéu, with a score of 2-6. It's good to remember that during those two seasons there were just four derbies, not because the calendar had less games, but because Real Madrid left the competitions it was involved in prematurely, in some cases in a humiliating way: in the Copa del Rey it didn't go beyond the 32-team round, eliminated by Real Unión (2008/09) and by Alcorcón (2009/10); and in the Champions it didn't go past the eighth-finals, surrendering to Liverpool (2008/09) – with an aggregate score of 5-0 (!) – and to Lyon (2009/10).

THE 'CASILLAS CASE'

Iker Casillas was born at the Bernabéu. He hadn't reached the age of ten yet when he wore the Merengue shirt for the first time. Any Madridista under 30 can't remember any structure in the Real Madrid goal other than the posts, the crossbar, the nets and... Iker.

He was promoted to captain, later canonised Saint Iker and thus won the title of 'immaculate' among the Merengue nation.

Casillas rose to the skies. He became omnipresent at the Bernabéu. He acquired more importance than any coach or even president of the Club. He was untouchable. Since he arrived at Real Madrid's pro team (1999/2000), he met 11 coaches (Vicente del Bosque, Carlos Queiroz, Camacho, García Remón, Luxemburgo, López Caro, Fabio Capello, Schuster, Juande Ramos, Pellegrini and Mourinho) and four presidents (Lorenzo Sanz, Florentino Pérez, Ramón Calderón and Vicente Boluda). A decade on the squad, practically always. Because saints don't make mistakes.

Only one coach, Vicente del Bosque, was able to take off his halo. Based on a strictly technical choice, the current Spanish national coach sat Casillas on the bench and fielded César, in the 2001/02 season. César's playing on the 'eleven' only ended in the 68th minute of the Champions final against Bayer Leverkusen, when the Cáceres goalkeeper was forced to stop because of an injury. Casillas went on and was instrumental in the 22 minutes he played, contributing decisively to winning the Champions League (1-2). His status of Saint was hugely reinforced.

Four years later, Fabio Capello also thought about sitting Iker. The Italian had always been suspicious of the goalkeeper's stature (1.82 m). On 14th October 2006 he confirmed his suspicion. In a League match against Getafe, at the Alfonso Pérez Coliseum, Casillas conceded a header goal from Alexis Ruano, from a dead-ball situation, which meant Real Madrid's defeat. Three days later, the Merengues had an important match in Bucarest, against Steaua, for the Champions League group stage. Capello almost chose the substitute goalkeeper called… Diego López (yes, him!), but he stuck with Casillas. Real Madrid won (1-4).

These two episodes show that, after all, despite all the Madridista beatification surrounding Iker Casillas, the goalkeeper from Madrid was not always object of consensus over the last decade. Before

Mourinho, others had already detected worrying technical short-comings. At least technical flaws.

WORRYING MISTAKES

The first red flag happened on 21st March 2012. El Madrigal, Villareal, League, 28th round, 83rd minute. Marcos Senna tied the match (1-1) by taking a frontal direct free kick. Casillas clearly badly beaten. A copy of what had happened three days before, against Málaga at the Bernabéu. Santi Cazorla also tied the match in the 92nd minute, with a free kick and the same collaboration of the Merengue goalkeeper. In a short of time, Iker Casillas made two identical mistakes and robbed Real Madrid of four precious points.

"I wish the best to Real Madrid and to Iker, but his mistakes are threatening the League. This is very serious! Iker Casillas is the best goalkeeper in the world but conceding the same type of goal twice in 72 hours is either lack of concentration or hubris", commented Hugo 'El Loco' Gatti, former professional goalkeeper. "These are unforgiveable mistakes. I don't know what is the problem of saying Iker conceded two goals and lost four points", the Argentine concluded, on the show "Punto Pelota", on Intereconomía TV. 'El Loco' was putting his finger on a wound that had been hidden by many for years. No-one compared to Iker Casillas between the goal posts, but away from them he revealed worrying shortcomings.

Being 'untouchable', a 'legend', a 'monument'... repeated countless times, these ratings took away Casillas' critical capacity, as well as that of the critics themselves. The technical team led by José Mourinho found a goalkeeper used to being on the squad and needing stimulus. The best remedy would be strong competition, which had actually already been equated and even attempted. Diego López had been a strong possibility, at the 2011/12 season kickoff, but his transfer fell through.

Ultimately, the four points awarded by Casillas to Málaga and Villarreal, on the 28th and 29th rounds, didn't compromise Real Madrid's winning the League. The matter 'Goalkeeper' was masked by the title, and postponed until the start of the 2012/13 season.

ABOVE THE GROUP

It would be unfair to handle the 'Casillas' issue merely on a technical plane. The truth is, in the Mourinho Era, Real Madrid won the 100-point League, reached two semi-finals of the Champions League and reconquered the Copa del Rey after 18 years. All this with Iker Casillas at the goal mouth. The disagreement between Mourinho and Casillas didn't just happen for technical reasons. That is to say, the technical reasons weren't even the most relevant part of the story.

"Problems happen when someone thinks he's above the group". This outburst by José Mourinho already in the last stretch of the season confirmed what everyone was suspecting. The Portuguese coach was referring to Iker Casillas and to his behaviour during Mourinho's three seasons in Madrid. This was the real reason for the rift between Mourinho and Casillas.

The spark was lit on 17th August 2011. The second leg of the Spain Supercup. A derby. The height of tension in the duels between Real Madrid and Barcelona. With a win of 3-2 at Camp Nou, Barça had just gained the trophy after the 2-2 tie at the Bernabéu. In the final minutes, 90+4, Marcelo sees a red card for bringing down Cesc Fàbregas by the touch line. The blancos protest, considering the Culer player put on an act. Trouble sets in at the benches, with pushes and aggressions from both sides. Never had a derby gone so far since Mourinho's arrival. The Real Madrid players didn't even wait for the trophy to be delivered. After the game, Iker Casillas spoke to TVE in the name of the group, to accuse the Barça players:

"I suppose trouble set in because of almost taking down an adversary, he threw himself to the floor… They always do that".

Just 24 hours later, Casillas regretted the declarations he'd made and felt the need to call two friends from Barcelona, Xavi and Puyol, explaining his mistake. Worse, he didn't inform Mourinho about the phone call and then made it public through Fernando Burgos. The Onda Cero journalist, a personal friend of Casillas, broke the news first-hand, catching the Portuguese coach totally off guard.

José Mourinho interpreted the team captain's behaviour as a breach of the team's spirit of solidarity and a betrayal to the hierarchy. It was even more serious because Casillas wore the armband, a symbol of his greater responsibility towards his colleagues. Casillas not only defused tensions with Real's main rival, but he made a point of making his gesture public, exposing the authority of the leader. Only the goalkeeper himself can explain the reasons for such an attitude.

Mourinho responded publicly to this episode a year and a half later, in May 2013, precisely with that idea: "Problems happen when someone thinks he's above all else, and with those, yes, obviously there are problems". But in practical terms, he gave his answer a few days after the Spanish Supercup. On 24th August 2011, Galatasaray was the guest of that year's edition of the Santiago Bernabéu Trophy. In a traditionally festive game, with the right to minutes for all players, Iker Casillas stayed on the bench throughout the 90 minutes, giving up his position to Antonio Adán. In fact, he was the only player, of the 22 called up, who wasn't used. The hint couldn't be more explicit. There was a leader and a discipline to comply with. Sacred, insurmountable principles for Mourinho. The first warning had been given.

A MONUMENT ON THE BENCH

The tug-of-war between José Mourinho and Iker Casillas was always present. Two days before Christmas 2012, the coach made the most drastic decision of all: to sit Iker Casillas on the substitutes' bench. It was during the match with Málaga, at La Rosaleda, for the League.

The topic 'Iker Casillas' dominated the Christmas break. The day after the game between Málaga and Real Madrid, which the Merengues lost 3-2, the capital's newspapers showed on page one the price that Mourinho would pay for challenging a legend: in the Marca, "Mou is being ridiculous"; in the As, "Challenge and failure. Punishment and penance". That same day, José Mourinho landed in Lisbon assuring he had a clear conscience, while Casillas took the opportunity, during a charity game called 'Game for illusion' taking place at the Madrid Sports Palace, to throw the first arrow: "I think I'm fine, but I'd already sensed I wasn't going to play".

The ice set in, for good, between both protagonists. The episodes that followed only served to confirm this. A month later, Sara Carbonero, Casillas' girlfriend, shattered whatever still remained. The TV presenter stated that the Real Madrid players were no longer with Mourinho and that the changing room was divided. A while later she referred to Cristiano Ronaldo as an "egotistic, self-absorbed" person. Luckily for everyone, the season only lasted three more months.

HOME IS WHERE THE HEART IS

It was this succession of episodes that made José Mourinho sigh for England, every day, during that last stretch of his career in Madrid. Mourinho wanted to win back the pleasure of working, breathe fresh air, and be able to go to restaurants or to walk in the streets without having to look over his shoulder.

Chelsea, an old passion, called him, and he went without hesitating... without ever looking back.

COMMITMENT LEADERSHIP

I don't know José Mourinho deeply. We've spoken, several times (I'm even owing him a visit to a training session, because he invited me), but we don't have a very close relationship. That's why my words are totally above suspicion.

However, in this case, I wouldn't need to have a close relationship or to watch Real Madrid training regularly to realise that not only has he got a good relationship with the players, but, above all, he has a professional commitment to them. And when a coach manages to communicate well with his players, they feel more protected, more comfortable and enjoy being there. On the other hand, the leader feels responsible and more committed to them.

A player's professional responsibility is just like a coach's. There has to be respect between them. And that he knows how to handle very well. I like that because I also feel that way. I'd like to have been coached by Mourinho. I really like that style: his capacity to establish complicities with the players; to be around them all the time; to defend them to the death, from everyone and everything. Because the real stars, those who solve the problems, those who win the championships, are the players. As coach, you just have to be with them.

A commitment has to exist. First the human relationship has to be as best as possible, because if there's a good personal relationship, professionally you can get the best performance out of the players. And he does that really well, not just in Real Madrid but in every team he's coached.

Organisation-wise, Mourinho introduced a new style that was different from what there was in Spain up to that moment. Until then, coaches simply coached players hired or suggested by other people. Mourinho implemented the English style in Real Madrid, assuming the position of manager. It makes total sense. If the coach is responsible for the results and results aren't good enough, his head will be the first to roll. I think it's a good idea for the coach to have the responsibility of suggesting contracts and, in that case, of structuring a team, like Alex Ferguson does in Manchester United, or Arsène Wenger in Arsenal. Mourinho worked for several years in England and he knows very well how this working method is beneficial for the team. He's managing to implement it in Real Madrid, which seemed quite difficult in a club like this.

But Mourinho's mission in Madrid is all but easy. He found his main rival, Barcelona, with a style well defined over decades, since the Cruyff era. That represents a huge advantage in football. In contrast, Mourinho arrived only a little over a year ago, and he needs time to achieve the results of his work and of his decisions. He's on the right track, things are better, the distance from Barcelona has become smaller and I think that perhaps this year it might be possible to end the reign in the League. Three years without winning the League is a long time for a club like Real Madrid. If we can add the Champions to the League, even better. But the League is a priority. And the following year, the Champions.

As I said, these won't be easy times for Mourinho. But I believe in his capacity and experience in dealing with difficult situations. His relationship with the media is a good example. The media have always liked controversy, because they have to sell. But Mourinho manages to 'distract' the press and public opinion, and take the pressure off the players. All this is done in a very intelligent way that few people even notice. He's intelligent; he knows how to handle the method of taking the pressure off the players, so that criticism, pressure and tension are placed upon him. That's really hard to do. This way, the players are free to focus on the only thing that matters: the match.

Real Madrid is the best club of all time and is used to having the best players and coaches in the world. But one thing is Real Madrid; another is the personality and character of the people working in Real Madrid so that the club continues to grow. You don't buy a club's image at the corner shop; you build it over many years and many successes. Real Madrid has its image, built with the help of all the players and coaches who worked there, and with all the titles won over the years. Whether it's Mourinho, Hugo Sanchéz or Di Stéfano who are there, Real Madrid will continue to be the greatest. It will continue to be the club where all the players and coaches want to be, because they know it's the greatest club in the world.

Everything that's said about Mourinho's posture or way of doing things, everything that's written about Mourinho's personality going against the values of Real Madrid, can only boil down to envy. Now Barcelona is in a good phase, but this is about cycles. This cycle is Barcelona's, but I think it'll end quickly with Mourinho around. Everything's going to change quickly with Mourinho.

HUGO SÁNCHEZ

TESTIMONIES

Dear José Mourinho, in professional football we meet people and then go separate ways. Three years ago you hired me for Real Madrid. In these three years you taught me a lot and fully trusted me. So today I want to thank you from the heart and wish you the best of luck in the future as coach. Thank you very much.

Mesut Özil

Mourinho is a good communicator and, more importantly, he's someone who doesn't cower. He knows which quick decisions he has to make to change the result of a match.

Xabi Alonso

I like people like him, outspoken, who say things to your face.

Arbeloa

He's the best coach I've had in my career. He's very professional, he supports you in every moment and he teaches you. That's essential for a football player.

Di Maria

Mourinho worked a lot with me on the mental factor of my game. Now I'm stronger in this respect. He's a great coach.

Karim Benzema

He's the best coach I've had and I can't find anyone better than him. He helps all the players advance. Tactically speaking, I progressed a lot with him. Mourinho made me a strategist.

Sami Khedira

I can only thank him and speak well of him. Thanks to Mourinho I have the opportunity to be in the first team of Real Madrid.

Nacho Fernández

SPECIAL MARKS...

Mourinho is the perfect coach.

SAMI KHEDIRA

Mourinho is arguably the best coach in the world.

PEP GUARDIOLA

TEAMS

Benfica (2000)
11 matches: 6 wins - 3 draws - 2 losses - 17|9 goals
League - 9 matches
Cup - 1 match
UEFA Cup - 1 match

União de Leiria (2001-2002)
20 matches: 9 wins - 7 draws - 4 losses - 34|20 goals
League - 19 matches
Cup - 1 match

FC Porto (2002-2004)
127 matches: 91 wins - 21 draws - 15 losses - 254|96 goals
League - 83 matches
Cup - 12 matches
Super Cup - 1
Champions League - 17 matches
UEFA Cup - 13 matches
European Super Cup - 1 match

Chelsea (2004-2007)
185 matches: 124 wins - 40 draws - 21 losses - 330|119 goals
League - 120 matches
FA Cup - 16 matches
League Cup - 13 matches
Super Cup - 3 matches
Champions League - 33 matches

Inter (2008-2010)
108 matches: 67 wins - 26 draws - 15 losses - 184|94 goals
League - 76 matches
Cup - 9 matches
Super Cup - 2 matches
Champions League - 21 matches

Real Madrid (2010-2013)
177 matches: 128 wins - 27 draws - 22 losses - 475|168 goals
League - 114 matches
Cup - 24 matches
Super Cup - 4 matches
Champions League - 36 matches

Total (2000-2013)

628 matches
425 wins (68%)
124 draws (20%)
79 losses (13%)
GF 1.294 (average 2,06) | GA 506 (average 0,81)

TITLES

7 National Championships

FC Porto (Portugal) 2002/03 and 2003/04
Chelsea (England) 2004/05 and 2005/06
Inter (Italy) 2008/09 and 2009/10
Real Madrid (Spain) 2011-12

4 National Cups

FC Porto (Portugal) 2002/03
Chelsea (England) 2006/07
Inter (Italy) 2009/10
Real Madrid (Spain) 2010/11

2 National League Cups

Chelsea (England) 2004/05 and 2006/07

3 National Super Cups

FC Porto (Portugal) 2002/03
Chelsea (England) 2004/05
Inter (Italy) 2008/09

2 Champions League

FC Porto (Portugal) 2003/04
Inter (Italy) 2009/10

1 UEFA Cup

FC Porto (Portugal) 2001/03

Individual awards

FIFA Golden Ball (2010); Coach of the year for UEFA (2003); Best coach in the world for FHEF (2004, 2005 and 2010); Coach of the year in Portugal (2002/03 and 2003/04); Coach of the year in England (2004/05 and 2005/06); Sports personality of the year for BBC (2005); Coach of the year in Italy (2008/09 and 2009/10); Calcio Oscar (2008/09 and 2009/10); Panchina d'Oro (2009/10);Best coach of the Spanish League newspaper Marca (2010/11); Best coach in the world for the International Sports Press Association (2010); Best coach in the world for the World Soccer Magazine (2004, 2005 and 2010)